BEST OF

Singapore

Charles Rawlings-Way

How to use this book

Colour-Coding & Maps

Each chapter has a colour code along the banner at the top of the page that is also used to indicate text and symbols on maps (eg all venues reviewed in the Highlights chapter appear orange on the maps). The fold-out maps inside the front and back covers are numbered from 1 to 6. All sights and venues in the text have map references; eg, (5, C1) means Map 5, grid reference C1. See p96 for map symbols.

Prices

Multiple prices listed with reviews (eg $10/5) usually indicate adult/child admission to a venue. Concession prices can include senior, student, member or coupon discounts. Meal cost and room rate categories are listed at the start of the Eating and Sleeping chapters, respectively.

Text Symbols

☎ telephone

✉ address

▯ email/website address

$ admission

☾ opening hours

ⓘ information

Ⓜ MRT (Mass Rapid Transit)

🚌 bus

♿ wheelchair access

✕ on site/nearby eatery

♿ child-friendly venue

Ⓥ good vegetarian selection

Best of Singapore
3rd edition – October 2006
First published – October 2002

Published by Lonely Planet Publications Pty Ltd
ABN 36 005 607 983

Australia Head Office, Locked Bag 1, Footscray, Vic 3011
☎ 03 8379 8000, fax 03 8379 8111
▯ talk2us@lonelyplanet.com.au
USA 150 Linden St, Oakland, CA 94607
☎ 510 893 8555, toll free 800 275 8555
fax 510 893 8572
▯ info@lonelyplanet.com
UK 72–82 Rosebery Ave, Clerkenwell, London
EC1R 4RW
☎ 020 7841 9000, fax 020 7841 9001
▯ go@lonelyplanet.co.uk

This title was commissioned in Lonely Planet's Melbourne office and produced by: **Commissioning Editors** Kalya Ryan and Jane Thompson **Coordinating Editors** Maryanne Netto and Martine Leonart **Coordinating Cartographers** Owen Eszeki and Natasha Velleley **Layout Designer** David Kemp **Managing Cartographer** Corinne Waddell **Cover Designer** Yukiyoshi Kamimura **Project Manager** Nancy Ianni **Thanks to** Melanie Dankel, Sally Darmody, Kusnandar, Katie Lynch, Suzannah Shwer and Celia Wood

Photographs by Lonely Planet Images and Glenn Beanland except for the following: p6, p12, p14, p23, p25, p28, p29, p30, p31, p34, p35, p40, p47, p48, p56, p58, p59, p63, p68, p70, p71, p79 Phil Weymouth; p53, p54, p55, p56, p57 Aun Koh; p8, p69 Michael Coyne; p37 Tom Cockrem; p5 Krzysztof Dydynski; p60 Alain Evrard; p9 Richard I'Anson; p77 Simon Richmond.
Cover photograph Chinese dragon dancers, Singapore National Day, Asia Photolibrary. All images are copyright of the photographers unless otherwise indicated. Many of the images in this guide are available for licensing from Lonely Planet Images: www.lonelyplanetimages.com.

ISBN 1 74059 911 X

Printed through The Bookmaker International Ltd.
Printed in China

Contents

From the Publisher

AUTHOR
Charles Rawlings-Way

Charles's earliest memories of Singapore are of being awestruck by air-conditioners and attempting to drown his father in the Hilton pool when he was seven. He's not as easily impressed or murderous these days, but Singapore still lures him back for regular pit stops.

A lapsed architect, shameless chilli addict and laksa aficionado, Charles greased the production wheels in Lonely Planet's Melbourne office for many years before making a break for the open road in 2005. Singapore, with its lapsed colonial architecture and chilli-laden laksa, made him feel right at home.

Thanks to the following folks for assistance great and small: Maryanne, Jules and Sam for your hospitality; Guy and Alice for your unexpected generosity; Miles, Zuly and Alexander for an indulgent few days; leisure consultants Dave and Lizzie Gregory; and Kalya Ryan.

A freelance writer, Charles lives with fellow Lonely Planet wordsmith Meg Worby among the virtue and vice of Melbourne's inner west.

The previous editions of this book was written by Rachael Antony.

LONELY PLANET AUTHORS

Why is our travel information the best in the world? It's simple: our authors are independent, dedicated travellers. They don't research using just the Internet or phone, and they don't take freebies in exchange for positive coverage. They travel widely, to all the popular spots and off the beaten track. They personally visit thousands of hotels, restaurants, cafés, bars, galleries, palaces, museums and more – and they take pride in getting all the details right, and telling it how it is. For more, see the authors section on **www.lonelyplanet.com**.

PHOTOGRAPHERS

Glenn Beanland

Born and raised in Melbourne, Australia, Glenn set out on his first photographic trip abroad in 1989. Since then he's travelled extensively and had images published by clients worldwide. He also works as a photo editor with Lonely Planet Images. He found Singapore was a fantastic city to photograph: 'It offered up a host of opportunities and rewarded the tired photographer's tastebuds with an unending array of local delicacies.'

Phil Weymouth

Australian born, Phil moved with his family to Iran in the late 1960s and called Tehran home until the revolution in 1979. He studied photography in Melbourne, returned to the Middle East to work as a photographer in Bahrain, then spent several years working for an Australian rural media company. He now runs a freelance photojournalism business based in Melbourne.

Although he had passed through Singapore countless times, when he had the chance to actually explore the city he found it was full of surprises: the Singapore River by water taxi, good cheap food from myriad cultures, and history that can sometimes be hidden by steel and glass.

SEND US YOUR FEEDBACK

We love to hear from travellers – your comments keep us on our toes and help make our books better. Our well-travelled team reads every word on what you loved or loathed about this book. Although we cannot reply individually to postal submissions, we always guarantee that your feedback goes straight to the appropriate authors, in time for the next edition – and the most useful submissions are rewarded with a free book. To send us your updates – and find out about Lonely Planet events, newsletters and travel news – visit our award-winning website: **www.lonelyplanet.com/feedback**.

Note: We may edit, reproduce and incorporate your comments in Lonely Planet products such as guidebooks, websites and digital products, so let us know if you don't want your comments reproduced or your name acknowledged. For a copy of our privacy policy visit **www.lonelyplanet.com/privacy**.

Introducing Singapore

City, island, nation – Singapore pivots on a delicate geographic, cultural and political fulcrum, just north of the Equator. Balancing deftly, the government directs society's traffic with utopian efficiency: graffiti-free trains run on time, crime is something you see on TV and traffic jams make front-page news.

Singaporeans traverse their city with blithe confidence, simmering in a strange brew of Chinese, Malay, Indian and Western cultures. Shopping is the national obsession; food the national treasure. Singapore can't match Bangkok's human circus, Tokyo's high-tech intensity or Sydney's great outdoors, but you get the feeling no-one really minds. Singapore addresses the world on its own terms and defends a self-satisfied equilibrium.

Guffawing critics ridicule this well-oiled 'Singabore', casting its good citizens as naive, skin-deep and unadventurous. Don't be deceived: the city's soul is subtle, slippery and irrepressible. Laced with juxtaposition, it shines through when you least expect it: incense drifts from a dutifully tended Buddhist shrine in an alley between high-rise hotels; a hyper-tensioned young executive discards a cigarette packet while an old man calmly folds recycled newspapers by the kerb; a punky, pierced teenager in a Metallica T-shirt sneers outside the Louis Vuitton shop window on Orchard Rd.

The Lion City is more than you bargained for – dust off your credit card, prime your stomach and gear up for some surprises.

Zipping around by water taxi on Singapore River

Precincts

Singapore is a diamond-shaped island some 45km west to east, 25km north to south. Downtown Singapore convenes around the Singapore River in the south, which, after decades in decline, has re-established itself as the city's watery heart. South of the river are the stalagmites of the CBD and the epicentre of Singapore's cultural life, **Chinatown** (Map 5). Immediately north of the river is the **Colonial District**, dappled with elegant colonial architecture, gargantuan shopping malls and the iconic Raffles Hotel. Lining the river itself are **Boat Quay**, **Clarke Quay** and **Robertson Quay**, once swampy, nefarious warehouse districts, now progressive entertainment and eating precincts. Visionary plans are afoot for redeveloping the **Marina Bay** area at the river mouth.

Most of Singapore's tourist action effervesces around Chinatown and along **Orchard Road**, just north of the Colonial District. Here also are the unfettered **Little India** and gracious **Kampong Glam**, Singapore's Islamic quarter.

East Coast Park stretches east from the city – imported sand on re-claimed land, it's hardly *The Blue Lagoon,* but it's a cool spot to chill out. Inland from here are the unpolished **Geylang** and **Katong** areas, the alleys off Geylang Rd harbouring Singapore's surprisingly saucy red-light district.

The much-lauded **Changi Airport** occupies the eastern corner of the island. North of here is **Changi Village**, from where you can hitch a bum-boat to the miraculously undeveloped **Pulau Ubin**. Diametrically opposed off Singapore's south coast, Ubin's cousin is the mega-touristy **Sentosa Island**.

In the centre of Singapore is a haven from the hype – a jewel-like tract of pristine rainforest, parkland and reservoirs, including the Bukit Timah Nature Reserve and MacRitchie Reservoir.

In a land dominated by high-rise architecture, Singaporean addresses are usually preceded by the number of the floor and then the shop or apartment number. For example, '03-12 Far East Plaza, Scotts Rd' is shop No 12 on the 3rd floor of Far East Plaza on Scotts Rd. Ground level is always called the 1st floor.

OFF THE BEATEN TRACK

Turn your back on Orchard Rd, the main tourist sights and organised tours and you'll quickly drift into calmer arenas. If you're craving some greenery, head for Bukit Timah Nature Reserve (p19), MacRitchie Reservoir (p28) or Pulau Ubin midweek. A morning or evening stroll along the river (p35) or East Coast Park (p28) can be surprisingly tranquil, or linger anonymously over a kick-ass Chinese coffee at a Little India or Kampong Glam coffee shop.

Itineraries

Singapore is a pocket-sized city with efficient and affordable public transport – there's no excuse for not covering a fair chunk of territory during your visit. The easiest and cheapest way to tackle the buses and trains is to get yourself an ez-link card (p83) from any MRT station (taxis are cheap too!). Eating is the essential Singaporean preoccupation – eat large, eat well, eat often.

Day One

Squander the morning on yum cha (bite-sized, savoury Chinese delights) in Chinatown, check out Thian Hock Keng Temple then head to HarbourFront for a cable car ride up Mt Faber and some magical views. Drift into the evening with a leisurely riverside stroll before succumbing to the least annoying restaurant spruiker on Boat Quay.

I-spy with my little eye…the cable car to Mt Faber

Day Two

Applaud some sporting efforts at the Padang, then check out the amazing Asian Civilisations Museum. Hit a hawker centre for a laksa (noodles in a spicy coconut soup) lunch, fortifying yourself for an Orchard Rd shopping spree followed by a sophisticated dinner and drinks an Chinatown's Club St.

Day Three

Shuffle through the morning in Little India and Kampong Glam, then go green at the Singapore Botanic Gardens, Bukit Timah Nature Reserve or the Singapore Zoo, working up an appetite for a pepper-crab feast at the East Coast Seafood Centre. Wind down with a show at the Esplanade, or wind up for some disco action at Zouk.

CHINATOWN (MAP 5)

Singapore's cherished cultural core is Chinatown, roughly bounded by Church St to the north, New Bridge Rd to the west, Maxwell Rd to the south and Cecil St to the east. It's a strange mix of ebullient commerce and sophisticated nightlife, tempered with memories of more desperate times when impoverished immigrants survived by their wits.

DON'T MISS

- Lunch at Yum Cha Restaurant (p50) and night-time hawker feasts
- Hip restaurants and bars along Club St
- Traditional teahouses and Chinese coffee shops
- Sri Mariamman Temple (p17)

The first Chinese arrived by junk in 1821, building the **Thian Hock Keng Temple** in thanks to sea goddess Ma Cho Po for a safe journey. Seeking opportunity and new beginnings, the reality for these settlers was a shock: torrid working conditions, lousy sanitation, disease, poverty, homesickness and opium addiction prevailed.

Sea breezes wafted through Chinatown before land reclamation shunted it a few blocks inland. A lot of the original architecture has been torn down and redeveloped over recent decades – **colonial shophouses** were regularly razed until the Urban Redevelopment Authority (URA) realised their heritage value and began wholesale renovations. Many traditional businesses have given way to tacky souvenir shops and upmarket restaurants, but entire shophouse strips have been saved and sumptuously restored.

Chinatown is stimulating, vibrant and tireless, from the Chinatown Complex's wet market and dusty medical halls to traditional bakeries, yum cha restaurants and – as yuppies make inroads – chic bars, designer stores and art galleries. Singapore sometimes feels like a city that's tried to bury its past, but Chinatown stands testament to what's never far below the surface.

INFORMATION

Ⓜ Chinatown, Tanjong Pagar, Outram Park

☒ see p49

Chinatown packed to the lanterns at dusk

ORCHARD ROAD (MAP 4)

Orchard Rd is a living shrine to the power of capitalism, globalisation, high disposable income and the modern belief that you are what you buy. But don't let that stop you from going shopping!

In the 19th century this stretch of road was lined with nutmeg and pepper plantations, traffic was strictly pedestrian and evening strolls were interrupted by the odd flood and tiger mauling. These days Orchard Rd is peppered with mega-malls, five-star hotels and soulless transnational franchises, with only a few remnants of former times: the Teutonic-inspired **Goodwood Park Hotel** on Scotts Rd, dating from 1900; the president's **Istana** (palace), former home of British governors; and a ramshackle strip of shophouses along **Emerald Hill Rd**.

Hectic at the best of times, Orchard Rd explodes into effervescent mayhem on weekends when Singaporeans swarm into shops and use the street like an extended lounge room. There's not much space or privacy in most HDB (Housing Development Board) flats, so the street is a hotspot for teenagers to hang out, compare ring-tones and canoodle.

Orchard Rd offers one of the world's densest **shopping** experiences: 7-Eleven stalls spray cooling mists over footpaths; models in impossibly slim-fit jeans shimmy out of Cartier and into Gucci; English Premier League football heroes scowl from house-high banners in sports-shop windows. Essential tools for survival: comfortable shoes, sharp elbows and a gold credit card.

INFORMATION

- ✉ Orchard Rd
- ⓘ Singapore Visitors Centre, cnr Cairnhill & Orchard Rds, open 9.30am-10.30pm
- Ⓜ Orchard, Somerset, Dhoby Ghaut
- ♿ good
- ✕ see p56

DON'T MISS

- Microboutiques by Singaporean designers at the Heeren (p41) and Level One (p41)
- Louis Vuitton shop window (p42)
- 40,000 sq ft of books at Kinokuniya (p46)
- Breakfast at Killiney Kopitiam (p57); Hainanese chicken rice at Chatterbox (p56)
- A drink at the Alley Bar (p61) on Emerald Hill Rd

LITTLE INDIA (3, E2)

Little India is worlds apart from the rest of Singapore. Originally a European enclave, the neighbourhood bloomed into an Indian cultural centre after a Jewish-Indian

INFORMATION
- Ⓜ Little India
- Ⓧ see p54

businessman started farming buffalo here. Today's Little India is true to its heritage: incense sticks and henna dyes jostle for space with baskets of dried chillies, jasmine garlands, technicolour sweets and gold-thread saris to a pumping Bollyrock soundtrack (so much sexier than Canto-pop twang).

Tourist groups trundle through on rickshaws, but this is a fairly detached experience – immerse your senses and explore on foot. At the **Tekka Centre wet market** crowds queue for biryani mutton (steamed basmati rice oven-baked with spices, meat and vegetables), *roti prata* (flaky, flat bread), brass knick-knacks and buckets of toads, wriggling mud crabs and bloody meat. **Little India Arcade** is touristy but good for souvenirs. **Clive Street, Dunlop Street** and **Campbell Lane** boast astrologers, traditional beauty treatments,

DON'T MISS
- Sri Veeramakaliamman Temple (p27)
- Souvenir shops selling saris, jewellery, spices and Bollyrock
- Banana-leaf curries and ginger tea
- A glass of wine at the French Stall (p55) for some quirky cross-cultural pollination

antiques, bangles and trinkets. **Kerbau Road** is taking off as an arts haven, with religious-art shops, galleries and performance groups. Oh, and did we mention the food? A paltry $3 will buy you a one-way ticket to curry nirvana. Top-notch budget accommodation adds spice to the pot.

The streets teem with men on two-year contracts from India, Bangladesh and Sri Lanka doing the dirty construction jobs Singaporeans won't stoop to. They might earn $50 a week here, compared to $5 back home. On Sunday evenings, thousands of these guys celebrate their day off, hanging out drinking, laughing and back-slapping. It's intense, unruly and very un-Singaporean!

Shops along Dickson Rd, Little India

ASIAN CIVILISATIONS MUSEUM (ACM) (3, D6)

This museum is a must for any Singapore visit – escape the humidity, put your watch in your pocket and enter a timeless realm.

Built in 1865, the imposing Empress Place building (named in honour of Queen Victoria) lived through various incarnations before the Singapore Tourism Board turned it into a museum in 1988. In 1992 the building was declared a national monument as part of the government's strategy for breathing life into Singapore's flagging cultural life. In 2002 the Asian Civilisations Museum opened its doors here, leaving the Singapore History Museum (renovations due for completion late 2006) for dead.

There are touring and special exhibitions in addition to the **10 thematic galleries**, set over three levels, exploring traditional aspects of pan-Asian culture and civilisation. The atmospherically lit interior shifts focus between exquisite, well-displayed artefacts from Southeast Asia, China, India, Sri Lanka and even Turkey, the emphasis on regions most strongly connected with Singapore's ethnic make-up. Japan is conspicuously absent, but we're

INFORMATION

☎ 6332 7798
🖳 www.nhb.govv.sg/acm
✉ 1 Empress Pl
💲 $8/4, after 7pm Fri admission free
🕑 1-7pm Mon, 9am-7pm Tue-Thu, Sat & Sun, 9am-9pm Fri
ⓘ information counter; free tours 2pm Mon, 11am & 2pm Tue-Fri, 11am, 2pm & 3.30pm Sat & Sun
Ⓜ Raffles Place, Clarke Quay
♿ good
✗ IndoChine Waterfront (p58)

assured this is due to the lack of Japanese cultural influence over Singapore, rather than any WWII misgivings. There's also a gallery examining Singapore's mercantile history along the Singapore River.

While there's been an attempt to contextualise the exhibits, unfortunately there's little meaningful curatorial connection made between the past and the present and, in keeping with the Singaporean way, the museum is politics-free. It is, however, refreshing to see Islam presented in a non-demonised way.

DON'T MISS

- Beautiful hand-inscribed Islamic scrolls and copies of the Qur'an
- Sumatran and Balinese gold and reproduction jewellery
- Hindu *vahana* (processional vehicles) in the South Asia gallery
- The winning rubber duck from the inaugural Singapore Million Dollar Duck Race, an annual rubber-duck charity race on the river
- A riverside drink at Bar Opiume (p61)

SINGAPORE ZOO & NIGHT SAFARI (2, D2)

The Singapore Zoo is world class. Set on a peninsula jutting into the Upper Seletar Reservoir, the zoo's 28 landscaped hectares are a far cry from the sad concrete confines some zoos retain.

There are more than 4000 residents here – 410 mammal, bird and reptile species – and most of them, with the possible exceptions of the polar bears and cheetahs, seem pretty happy. Endangered species include Komodo dragons, malodorous white rhinos, a charismatic orang-utan colony, and blue-eyed white tigers with paws as big as your face. The zoo claims to have the world's largest primate collection – if you visit on a weekend, the sweaty human hordes doing the rounds blur the distinctions between man and ape.

Newer attractions such as the Australian Outback exhibit and the Hamadryas Baboons – The Great Rift Valley of Ethiopia enclosure convey entire ecosystems: animal, mineral, vegetable and human. Visitors can stand behind a window in 'Ethiopia' and watch 50 shameless red-bummed baboons doing things that Singaporeans still get arrested for.

INFORMATION
- ☎ 6269 3411
- 🖳 www.zoo.com.sg
- ✉ 80 Mandai Lake Rd
- 💲 zoo $15/7.50, zoo tram $4/2, night safari $20/10, night-safari tram $6/3, combined zoo & safari $28/14
- 🕑 zoo 8.30am-6pm; night safari 7.30pm-midnight (restaurants from 6.30pm)
- ⓘ information desk, volunteer night-safari rangers
- Ⓜ Ang Mo Kio then bus 138 or Choa Chu Kang then bus 927
- ♿ good
- ✖ or bring a picnic

ANIMALIA
Surprisingly, Singapore is home to 300 native bird species, otters, monitor lizards, pit vipers, king cobras and 10m-long reticulated pythons. Malayan tigers and clouded leopards prowled Singapore's jungles until the early 1900s; smaller leopard cats still sometimes surprise the pants off someone, but you're more likely to see macaques (monkeys) and squirrels.

Want more beast for you buck? Visit the zoo in the late afternoon then hit the **Night Safari** next door. Clamber aboard the tram for an atmospheric jungle ride past a parade of spotlit nocturnal species. Things

Big fan of fruit; not so fond of the big durian

can be a bit hit-and-miss here – a lot depends on your tram conductor's sense of humour and whether or not the animals come out to play. The impressive Creatures of the Night show (8pm, 9pm and 10pm) will make you wonder why we ever bothered to evolve.

ESPLANADE – THEATRES ON THE BAY (3, D6)

Architecturally out-of-this-world, the Esplanade arts and theatre development opened in 2002, the cornerstone of a government programme to turn Singapore into an arts hub. Aiming for the same impact as the Sydney Opera House, the architects wanted to challenge ingrained Singaporean conservatism, and they sure pushed the right buttons – the centre has been compared to flies' eyes, melting honeycomb, two upturned durians and called a whole lot of rude words we can't repeat here.

The Esplanade was built on reclaimed waterfront land at a cost of $600 million. It took two years to prepare the site to support the building (the entire structure sits on an enormous rubber slab); then, strangely, the theatres were built from the inside out. The controversial exterior is an assembly of variously angled aluminium shades, the shapes of which reference natural geometries and traditional Asian reed weavings, maximising natural light while shielding the glass roof from the sun. At night, internal lighting sets the building aglow. The integral Esplanade shopping mall feels like a bit of an add-on, but has some great restaurants and views across Marina Bay.

Whatever you think of the design, there's no doubting the Esplanade's success as an arts venue, with a nonstop programme of international and local dance, opera, classical music, jazz, cultural festivals, puppetry, recitals, installations and exhibitions wowing the masses. Most tickets can be booked in advance through **SISTIC** (☎ 6348 5555; www.sistic.com.sg).

INFORMATION

- ☎ 6828 8377
- 🖳 www.esplanade.com
- ✉ 1 Esplanade Dr
- $ admission free, guided tours $8/5, prices for shows variable
- ☺ arts centre 7am-late, box office noon-8.30pm, mall 11am-9.30pm, restaurants 11am-late
- ⓘ information desk; guided tours 11am & 2pm Mon-Fri, 11am Sat & Sun
- Ⓜ City Hall
- ♿ good
- ✖ My Humble House (p58-9)

DURIAN DURIAN

The Esplanade's durian comparisons are architecturally insulting, not because durians look particularly ugly but because they smell like decaying socks. Their aroma is so funky that durians are banned from MRT trains, but they're actually pretty tasty – something like sweet buttery custard. Try one – we dare you!

SINGAPORE BOTANIC GARDENS (2, E4)

It sounds like an experiment from *Frankenstein*, but 'Connecting Plants with People' is the Botanic Gardens' catch cry. Wide green spaces like these are rare in Singapore – perfect for jetlag recovery, picnics, reading a paper or just wandering around aimlessly.

ORCHID OBSESSION

Singapore loves orchids – the national flower is the Vanda Miss Joaquim orchid, orchid displays are hotel lobby mainstays, and there are a staggering 30,000 species and 100,000 hybrids cultivated here. With delicate stems and reluctant petals, orchids seem like fragile beauties, but they're actually one of the world's hardiest plants, coping equally well in desert or rainforest.

Established around 1860 and covering 52 hectares, the gardens were originally a laboratory for potential cash crops such as rubber and coffee. Today they host a herbarium with more than 600,000 specimens, and a library of archival materials dating back to the 16th century. Meander through the frangipani collection, the Evolution Garden's pre-historic plants or plunge into the 4-hectare 'original Singaporean jungle', a small slice of the kind of rainforest that once blanketed the island. Maintenance brigades in red jump suits patrol with mowers, blowers and trimmers to keep the jungle at bay; pre-wedding photographers dab beads of sweat from nervous grooms' brows. At night, boughs are up-lit for magical effect.

The **National Orchid Garden** is also here, with over 60,000 plants and a 'cool house' showcasing orchids from cooler climes. Cool! Hype aside, orchids are extraordinary beasts, worth a look even if you don't really, ahem, dig flowers.

The gardens host free open-air music concerts on the first Sunday of the month at the Shaw Foundation Symphony Stage – call the gardens or the Singapore Tourism Board for details.

INFORMATION

- ☎ 6471 7361
- 🖥 www.sbg.org.sg
- ✉ 1 Cluny Rd
- 💲 admission free, National Orchid Garden $5/1
- 🕐 5am–midnight, National Orchid Garden 8.30am–7pm
- ℹ information desk at entrance; call to arrange tours
- 🚌 7, 105, 123, 174, 502
- ♿ good
- 🍴 Café Les Amis (at main entrance), Halia (p56), Au Jardin Les Amis (p56)

THIAN HOCK KENG TEMPLE (5, C2)

Also known as the Temple of Heavenly Happiness, this is one of Singapore's oldest and most eye-popping temples. Dedicated to Ma Cho Po, goddess of the sea, it was built on a joss house site between 1839 and 1942 by early Hokkien immigrants from China in gratitude for safe passage to Singapore. It's hard to imagine now, but this was once a waterfront temple; Telok Ayer St was the centre of Chinatown's commerce and slave trade before land reclamation shifted the shore 500m east.

Architecturally faithful to 19th-century Chinese design, Thain Hock Keng adheres to the principles of feng shui with open internal courtyards surrounded by pavilions. No expense was spared in its construction: the **statue of Ma Cho Po** was shipped from China's Fukien Province in 1840, decorative tiles were imported all the way from Holland, and cast-iron railings brought from Scotland. It was built using traditional joinery (no nails!) by super-skilled Chinese artisans.

Declared a National Monument in 1973 and renovated in 2000, the temple's twin rooftop dragons

INFORMATION

- ☎ 6423 4616
- 🖥 www.shhk.com.sg
- ✉ 158 Telok Ayer St
- 💲 free
- 🕐 7.30am-5.30pm
- Ⓜ Chinatown, Tanjong Pagar
- ✖ Chinatown (p49)

Decorative drum at Thian Hock Keng Temple

CHINESE TEMPLES

Buddhist, Taoist or Confucian, many Chinese temples have similar features. Outside there's usually a furnace where prayers, incense and ghost money (afterlife currency) are burnt. Screens separate the entrance from the main hall's deities; funerary tablets have a separate room. Be respectful: remove your shoes and only photograph sculptures and architecture.

represent the principles of yin and yang. Two stone lions guard the door, and – as security back-up – fierce-looking portraits of door gods prevent evil spirits from entering. Inside, gilded ceilings feature intricate carvings of Chinese folkloric stories and heroes, while suitably awestruck school tour groups light incense at shrines dedicated to Bao Sheng Da Di (life-protector), Guan Ti (god of war) and Yue Gong Niang Niang (moon goddess).

RAFFLES HOTEL (3, D5)

It's one of the most hyped hotels in the world, but no matter how you look at it, there's only one Raffles. Singapore has been all too eager to distance itself from its colonial past, but Raffles has survived – an adored Singaporean institution and refined architectural landmark.

Raffles Hotel started life in 1887 as a 10-room bungalow, but the good times didn't really start to roll until the main building opened in 1899. Raffles soon became synonymous with Oriental opulence, enticing colonial literary giants including Joseph Conrad, Somerset Maugham, Rudyard Kipling and Noel Coward to its breezy balconies. Other claims to fame include the invention of the **Singapore Sling** here by bartender Ngiam Tong Boon, and the inglorious shooting of the last Singaporean tiger beneath the Billiard Room in 1902.

Linen-suited decadence was suddenly put on ice when the

INFORMATION

- ☎ 6337 1886
- 🖳 www.raffleshotel.com
- ✉ 1 Beach Rd
- 💲 rooms $750-4500
- Ⓜ City Hall
- ♿ good
- ✘ see p52

There's no cost to look...Raffles Hotel

SINGAPORE SLING

Sipping a Singapore Sling in Raffles' Long Bar and throwing peanut shells on the floor is a quintessential Singapore experience. A frosty glass of the sweet, cherry-red delight will set you back around $20, or collate your duty-free bottles and whip one up yourself:

- 30ml gin
- 15ml cherry brandy
- 120ml pineapple juice (or soda)
- 15ml lime juice
- 10ml Cointreau orange liqueur
- 10ml Benedictine herbal liqueur
- 15ml Angostura bitters

Shake it up with ice then strain into a highball glass; top with a cherry and a slice of pineapple.

Japanese invaded during WWII and demanded room service. After the war the hotel became a transit camp for liberated Allied prisoners, by which time the glamour days were well and truly over.

In 1987 Raffles was narrowly saved from the demolition ball when the government declared it a protected monument. A $160-million facelift ensued, complete with high-brow shopping mall, restaurants, cooking school, day spa and museum. Most ordinary mortals can't afford to stay here, but take a wander through the courtyards, past fountains and rattling palms and imagine that tigers are still on the prowl.

SRI MARIAMMAN TEMPLE (5, C1)

Paradoxically cast in the middle of Chinatown, the Sri Maria... ple is the oldest Hindu temple in Singapore. You can't miss the incredible technicolour *gopuram* (tower) above the entrance, key to the temple's South-Indian Dravidian style. Sacred cow sculptures graze along the temple's boundary walls, while the 1930s *gopuram* is covered in over-the-top plasterwork images of that potent Hindu trio: Brahma the creator, Vishnu the preserver and Shiva the destroyer. The actual temple is dedicated to the healing goddess Sri Mariamman, a favourite among Tamils for her rain-bringing inclinations and knack for curing what ails you – a clue to the tough conditions Singapore endured in the 1800s.

Naraina Pillai, a trader who arrived in Singapore with Sir Stamford Raffles, first built a wooden temple here in 1827. The present stone building dates from 1862, though it's undergone countless renovations since then, usually in preparation for consecration ceremonies which happen every 12 years.

Far from the madding Pagoda and Smith St crowds, worshippers offer initial prayers at the **Shrine of Sri Vinayagar** – lord of beginnings and remover of obstacles – before presenting offerings (anything from fruit and incense to mouthwash mints) to other deities, or retreating to pray quietly in shadowy alcoves. Only the loincloth-clad priests are allowed to enter the temple's inner sanctum, where they bathe statues in coloured waters.

JUST GOOD FRIENDS

Confident in their masculinity, it's standard practice for Indian and Bangladeshi foreign workers to walk around holding hands with their male friends, leaning on each others shoulders on street corners and being openly affectionate. Conversely, you'll rarely – if ever – see a local Indian man being as demonstrative with friends and family in public.

In October each year the temple hosts the **Thimithi Festival** – devotees queue along South Bridge Rd to hot-foot it over burning coals.

Sri Mariamman Temple's *gopuram*

INFORMATION

- ☎ 6223 4064
- ▯ www.visitsingapore.com
- ✉ 244 South Bridge Rd
- $ admission free, photography/ video cameras $3/6
- ◷ 7.30am-8.30pm
- ⓘ English brochure available at the door ($1)
- Ⓜ Chinatown
- ♿ fair
- ✕ Chinatown (p49)

BOAT QUAY & CIRCULAR ROAD (3, C6)

Loud, tacky and sometimes ugly, Boat Quay is a mainstream tourist magnet, exploiting incoming dollars from unadventurous travellers. That said, there are few prettier places for dinner in Singapore, and there are some great restaurants here. The trick to getting the best out of Boat Quay is to reserve your table in advance; don your thick skin, smile and run the gauntlet of overzealous restaurant spruikers. Order some wine and watch the wake from chugging bumboats ripple the reflections on the river.

Chinese *towkay* (trader chiefs) originally moored here because the riverbank's gentle arc resembles a carp's belly – a sign of good fortune. By the 1860s, three quarters of Singapore's shipping business was being transacted here. The swampy riverbank consolidated into a quay, boats moored seven and eight deep, with many godown (warehouses) that supported the vigorous trade. By the 1960s Singapore's shipping had shifted to deeper waters, and Boat Quay sank into disrepair. Revived during the 1980s and '90s, most of today's picturesque shophouses date from the 1930s.

INFORMATION

- ✉ Boat Quay & Circular Rd
- $ admission free, club cover-charges vary
- ☺ 11am-late
- Ⓜ Clark Quay, Raffles Place
- ♿ fair
- ✖ The Quays (p58)

OH BEHAVE!

Boat Quay and Circular Rd can get raucous, but Singaporeans are generally a civilised bunch. Billboards instruct citizens on the finer points of courtesy, graciousness and public decency – 'Value life, act responsibly' is the creed, with a generous serve of 'Have a nice day'. Eight-year-old kids catch the train by themselves; women walk unconcerned at night. How refreshing!

Parallel to Boat Quay one block to the south is Circular Rd, which, due to a relaxation of liquor licensing laws, has exploded as a nightlife strip. Literally dozens of new bars have opened here in the past few years, luring thirsty after-work businessmen from the CBD just a few blocks away. There are 24-hour beer bars, dance clubs, karaoke bars, an Irish Pub, a refrigerated 'ice' bar and plenty of cheap eats to soak it all up.

Fancy a pint anyone?...Boat Quay watering holes

BUKIT TIMAH NATURE RESERVE (2, D3)

Singapore's steamy heart of darkness is Bukit Timah Nature Reserve, a 164-hectare tract of primary equatorial rainforest – the last undeveloped pocket of the island's original jungle – clinging to the slopes of Singapore's highest peak, Bukit Timah (163.63m). Established as a reserve in 1883 at the far-sighted recommendation of Nathaniel Cantley, then superintendent of the Singapore Botanic Gardens, Bukit Timah has never been logged. The closest it's come to human domination was as a strategic battle point during the WWII Japanese invasion.

Florid British naturalist David Bellamy once pointed out that a measly hectare of Bukit Timah holds more tree species than the entire North American continent. The unbroken forest canopy also shelters what remains of Singapore's native wildlife, including obnoxious long-tailed macaques (monkeys), the occasional slithering python and birds ranging from greater racquet-tailed drongos to white-bellied sea eagles.

INFORMATION

- ☎ 1800 468 5736
- 🖥 www.nparks.gov.sg
- ✉ 177 Hindhede Dr
- $ free
- 🕒 7am-7pm, visitors centre 8.30am-6pm
- ℹ visitors centre (at the entrance of Hindhede Dr)
- Ⓜ Orchard, then bus 171
- 🚌 75 from CBD, 170 from Queen St Bus Terminal
- ✗ drinks only (at visitors centre)

It's OK to feed the children

There are four well-established **walking trails** through the reserve, from 20 minutes to one hour return. For a distinctly out-of-Singapore experience, tackle the challenging North View, South View or Fern Valley paths, involving some scrambling over rocks and tree roots. There are also 6km of **cycling trails** circumnavigating the forest. Pick up a trail map from the visitors centre; check out the exhibition space while you're there.

The steep paths are sweaty work, so take plenty of water, embalm yourself in mosquito repellent, and don't feed the monkeys no matter how politely they ask.

WELCOME TO THE JUNGLE

To paraphrase Robin Williams in *Good Morning Vietnam*, Singapore is 'HOT and WET. That's nice if you're with a lady, but ain't no good if you're in the jungle...'. Surrounded by concrete, it's easy to ignore Singapore's natural state, but butterflies, buttress roots and scampering geckoes hint at the patiently lurking jungle – don't feel too secure!

SENTOSA ISLAND (MAP 1)

One person's highlight is another's loathsome lowlight – in the case of Sentosa it somehow manages to be both. The Brits turned this tiny isle at the southern tip of Singapore into a military fortress in the late 1800s. In 1967 it was returned to the government, which developed it into a holiday resort.

The Sentosa philosophy is 'too much is never enough' – the only way to survive is to suspend cynicism, embrace garishness and launch yourself into it with a vengeance. The island is plastered with a bewildering array of tourist attractions, ranging from the absurdly overblown **Merlion** with its sea monster displays, to the **Musical Fountain**, which projects visitors' sincerest love messages onto a water-screen. **Underwater World** will distract the kids with sharks, dugongs and crustaceans, while the **Images of Singapore** and **Fort Siloso** museums offer some substance for grown-ups to chew on. The **Carlsberg Sky Tower** and bone-rattling **Sentosa Luge** will keep everybody entertained.

Alternatively, shun the attractions and stick to nature: explore the **Dragon Trail Nature Walk**, check out the **Butterfly Park**, hire a mountain bike, or head for one of Sentosa's three **beaches** – the imported sand, fake boulders and piped tin-drum renditions of *Girls Just Wanna Have Fun* and *Summer Holiday* are something to cherish. You can also play volleyball, soccer or golf, hire a kayak, or just kick back on the island's improving crop of restaurants and bars.

Love it or hate it, there's nowhere in the world quite like Sentosa.

INFORMATION

- ☎ 1800 736 8672, emergency/ranger 6279 1155
- 🖳 www.sentosa.com.sg
- ✉ Sentosa Island
- 💲 admission $2, Sentosa bus return per passenger $1, per car $2, attractions from $8/5, multiattraction packages from $25.90/17.90
- 🕓 bus 7am-11pm Sun-Thu, 7am-12.30am Fri & Sat, cable car 8.30am-11pm, hours for attractions vary
- ⓘ information counters at bus and cable car terminals
- Ⓜ HarbourFront, then Sentosa bus or cable car (return $10.90/5.50)
- ♿ fair
- ✗ several restaurants on the island

SENTOSA ON FOOT

Sentosa has four colour-coded bus lines zooming between attractions, and motorised trams connecting the beaches. Theoretically it's pedestrian-friendly, but footpaths are intermittent, it's steep, hot and sticky, and you'll get some curious looks from air-conditioned tourist busloads as you stomp around. You can walk across the bridge to the island, but no-one ever does – reason enough to do it!

MT FABER (2, E5)

Mt Faber stands proud (if not tall) at 116m on the southern fringe of the city, opposite the Harbour-Front Centre and not far from Sentosa Island. From the summit, the strange splendour of Singapore rolls away to the horizon in all directions. To the south is the port with its giant cranes and sinister-looking smoke plumes, beyond which the Strait of Singapore seethes with hundreds of ships at anchor. To the north lies the city, the river, and a morass of high-rise HDB apartment towers, teetering in to the base of Mt Faber.

INFORMATION

- ☎ 6377 9688
- 🖳 www.mountfaber.com.sg
- ✉ 109 Mt Faber Rd
- 💲 admission free
- 🕒 cable car 8.30am-11pm
- ℹ information desk at summit
- Ⓜ HarbourFront, then cable car (one-way $9.90/4.50)
- 🚌 shuttles from HarbourFront bus terminal (6pm-3am Mon-Fri, 7am-3am Sat & Sun)
- 🍴 Altivo, Sky Dining (p30)

To get to the top, ride the spectacular **cable car** from HarbourFront, take the shuttle bus, or gear up for the climb from the bottom. The flanks of the hill, err, mountain, are steeply terraced, so there's not much room for lolling around off the pathways, but the maze of trails takes you through twisted copses of dense, buzzing forest, with strategically positioned seats, pavilions and lookouts along the way. **Faber Point**, just west of the cable car terminus, is a tranquil, less contrived spot to soak up the views (binoculars for three minutes $1).

KAMPUNG DAYS

Fifty years ago the view from Mt Faber would have been vastly different. Until the 1950s, most Singaporeans lived in single-storey homes in their *kampung* (traditional Malay village), but population pressures and land scarcity demanded change. Singaporeans remain sentimental about the *kampung*, but 90% of them now live in HDB high-rise apartments – a phenomenal turnaround!

Singapore's *Cosmo* magazine voted Mt Faber's Altivo lounge bar one of the best places for after-dark romanticisms – the perfect spot to watch the sun set over the straits. Unless cable car key-rings are your heart's desire, pretend the tacky souvenir shop next door doesn't exist.

Play count-the-highrise from Mt Faber

MUSEUMS

See also the Asian Civilisations Museum (p11). Closed for renovation at the time of research, the Singapore History Museum (3, C4) was due to reopen in late 2006.

Battle Box (3, C4)
Iside Fort Canning Hill, Battle Box is the site of Singapore's largest WWII underground military complex. War veterans and Britain's Imperial War Museum helped recreate the authentic bunker environs; life-sized models re-enact the surrender to Japan on 15 February 1942.
☎ 6333 0510; fax 6333 0590 ✉ 51 Canning Rise 💲 $8/5 ⏲ 10am-6pm Ⓜ Dhoby Ghaut ♿ fair

Changi Museum & Chapel (2, H3)
Adjoining the prison, Changi Museum poignantly commemorates WWII Allied POWs who suffered horrific treatment at the hands of invading Japanese. Stories are told through photographs, letters, drawings and murals; tales of heroism and celebration of peace lighten the mood.
☎ 6214 2451 💻 www.changimuseum.com ✉ 1000 Upper Changi Rd North 💲 admission free, tours $8/4 ⏲ 9.30am-5pm Ⓜ Tanah Merah, then bus 2 ♿ good

Chinatown Heritage Centre (5, B1)
On three floors of an old shophouse, this engaging museum focuses on the arduous everyday lives of Singapore's Chinese settlers. Reconstructed environments are festooned with artefacts, the 'four evils' – gambling, prostitution, secret societies and opium addiction – lurking in every corner.
☎ 6325 2878 💻 www.chinatownheritage.com.sg ✉ 48 Pagoda St 💲 $8.80/5.30 ⏲ 9am-8pm Mon-Thu, 9am-9pm Fri-Sun Ⓜ Chinatown

Malay Heritage Centre (3, E3)
This terracotta-tiled museum was once the Malay royal Istana (palace), built in 1843 for Singapore's last sultan. Celebrating Singapore's Malay heritage, there's a reconstructed *kampung* (village) house, with cultural performances ($10/5) at 3pm Wednesday and 11.30am Sunday.
☎ 6391 0450 💻 www.malayheritage.org.sg ✉ 85 Sultan Gate 💲 $3/2 ⏲ 10am-6pm Tue-Sun, 1-6pm Mon Ⓜ Bugis ♿ ground level only

Raffles Museum (3, D5)
You could easily dismiss this place as an exercise in self-aggrandisement, but it's actually very interesting. Old photos and advertisements rub shoulders with reminiscences from celebrity guests such as Somerset Maugham. Don't miss the 1910 Singapore River photo-panorama.
☎ 6337 1886 💻 www.rafflehotel.com ✉ 03 Raffles Hotel, 1 Beach Rd 💲 free ⏲ 10am-10pm Ⓜ City Hall ♿ good

---

MONUMENTAL ACHIEVEMENTS
Keep an eye out for these monuments as you're cruising the streets:

- Alkaff Bridge (3, B6) – inspired by bumboats (but more like a banana on acid), this technicolour bridge at Robertson Quay was painted by Filipino artist Pacita Abad in 2004.
- Civilian War Memorial (3, D5) – aka 'The Chopsticks', these four pillars at the War Memorial Park represent the Chinese, Eurasian, Indian and Malay civilian casualties of the WWII Japanese invasion.
- Merlion (3, D6) – Singapore's funky water-spouting icon at Merlion Park; half-lion, half-fish (below).
- Raffles Landing Site (3, D6) – at North Boat Quay is this modern version of the original bronze statue (now outside the Victoria Concert Hall) where Stamford stepped into the mud.

Raffles Museum (opposite)

Singapore Art Museum
(3, D4)

Formerly the St Joseph's Institution Catholic boys school, the Art Museum champions the arts in an economics-obsessed nation. Exhibitions range from classical Chinese calligraphy to electronic arts; contemporary works examine Southeast Asian identity and the modern Singaporean condition. Tours in English 11am and 2pm daily.
☎ 6332 3222 ▯ www .museum.org.sg/nhb ✉ 71 Bras Basah Rd $ $3/1.50, 6-9pm Fri free ☾ 10am-7pm Sat-Thu, 10am-9pm Fri Ⓜ City Hall ♿ good

Civilian War Memorial

Singapore City Gallery
(5, C2)

The Urban Redevelopment Authority (URA) gallery provides an insight into the government's hell-bent policies of high-rise housing and land reclamation. Highlights include an 11m x 11m scale model of the city, a cheesy 'Know Your Singapore' audio-visual display, and a voyeuristic bird's-eye-view roof camera.
☎ 6321 8321 ▯ www .ura.gov.sg/gallery ✉ URA Centre, 45 Maxwell Rd $ free ☾ 9am-5pm Mon-Sat Ⓜ Tanjong Pagar ♿ good

BUILDINGS & MONUMENTS

See also Esplanade – Theatres on the Bay (p13), Fullerton Hotel (p71) and Raffles Hotel (p16).

Carlsberg Sky Tower
(1, B2)

Looking like a camembert impaled on a carrot, the Sky Tower is one of Sentosa Island's newer tourist magnets. Take the slow ride up the 131m column for some superb Singapore views. More terrifying is the prospect of the 'Carlsberg Float' – its beer and ice-cream monstrosity.
☎ 1800 736 8672 ▯ www .sentosa.com.sg ✉ Sentosa Island $ $10/6 ☾ 9am-9pm Ⓜ to HarbourFront, then bus or cable car ➡ see Sentosa Island p20 ♿ good

CHIJMES (3, D5)

Refined CHIJMES was founded in 1854 as the Convent of the Holy Infant Jesus, functioning as an orphanage and school until 1983. These days it's a mosaic of restaurants, bars, shops, fountains and quiet cobbled walkways – a tranquil change from the streets.
☎ 6338 2529 ▯ www .chijmes.com.sg ✉ 30 Victoria St $ free ☾ 11am-late Ⓜ City Hall ♿ good

Courtyard at CHIJMES

Istana (3, B2)

Built in the 1860s at huge expense (to impress the visiting Duke of Edinburgh), the neo-Palladian Istana (palace) is where Singapore's President SR Nathan hangs out. It's only open to the public on selected holidays (eg New Year's) – bring your passport to get past the gun-toting guards.
☎ 6737 5522 ▯ www .istana.gov.sg ✉ Orchard Rd $ free ☾ selected holidays only Ⓜ Dhoby Ghaut

Kranji War Cemetery
(2, D2)

These austere white structures and rolling lawns contain the WWII graves of thousands of Allied troops. Walls are inscribed with the names of 24,346 people who died in Southeast Asia. Register books are available for inspection.
☎ 9269 6158 ▯ www .cwgc.com ✉ 9 Woodlands Rd $ free ☾ 24hr Ⓜ Kranji, then bus 170

GALLERIES

Too often driven by market opportunity rather than artistic vision, the Singapore gallery scene is nonetheless vibrant. Many galleries are closed on Sunday and/or Monday; those listed below are free. See also the Singapore Art Museum (p23).

Art-2 Gallery (3, C5)

One of the excellent galleries in the rainbow-shuttered MICA building, Art-2 zooms in on contemporary Southeast Asian sculpture, featuring regional ceramicists and painters including Wang Meng Leng and Poh Siew Wah.
☎ 6338 8719 ▯ www .art2.com.sg ✉ 01-03 MICA Bldg, 140 Hill St ⌚ 11am-7pm Mon-Sat Ⓜ Clarke Quay Ⓖ fair

Art Seasons (5, C2)

This 'trendy' (Singapore's favourite adjective) three-storey commercial gallery exhibits and sells cool and quirky contemporary work (mainly paintings) by Singaporean and regional artists. It also showcases contemporary Burmese artists.
☎ 6221 1800 ▯ www .artseasons.com.sg ✉ The Box, 5 Gemmill La ⌚ 11am-8pm Mon-Fri, noon-7pm Sat Ⓜ Chinatown

Boon's Pottery (4, A3)

A gallery-shop hybrid, this slightly offbeat place sells a broad range of beautiful ceramics made with local clays. Owner Chuan Siang Boon makes a habit of donating works to bigwigs like Bill Gates and the Singapore Police Force.
☎ 6836 3978; fax 6836 3979 ✉ 01-30 Tanglin Mall, 163 Tanglin Rd ⌚ noon-9pm Mon-Sat Ⓜ Orchard ▯ 7, 77, 106, 111, 174 Ⓖ good

Plastique Kinetic Worms (3, D2)

Looking for something off-the-wall for your wall? This is where you'll get it. Singapore's only artist-run, nonprofit gallery promotes the works of young and contemporary conceptual artists who find it hard to exhibit in more commercial spaces.
☎ 6292 7783 ▯ www.pk worms.org.sg ✉ 61 Kerbau Rd ⌚ 11am-7pm Tue-Sun Ⓜ Little India Ⓖ fair

Sculpture Square (3, D4)

Resonating arty vibes through a gothic Methodist chapel (built 1870–75), Sculpture Square is a nonprofit gallery exhibiting works by Singaporean artists, including Han Sai Por (check out his *Seed* sculptures along the Esplanade waterfront).

Contemporary sculpture and 3-D art are the focus, with year-round sculpture workshops.
☎ 6333 1055 ▯ www .sculpturesq.com.sg ✉ 155 Middle Rd ⌚ 11am-6pm Mon-Fri, noon-6pm Sat & Sun Ⓜ Bugis Ⓖ fair

Sculpture Square

Singapore Tyler Print Institute (3, B6)

This white-walled, polished concrete space hosts international and local exhibits, showcasing the work of resident print and paper makers. Exhibitions often have a 'how to' component, and there's an impressive programme of visual arts courses year-round.
☎ 6336 3663 ▯ www .stpi.com.sg ✉ 02-41 Robertson Quay ⌚ 10am-6pm Tue-Sat ▯ 51, 64, 123 all to Havelock Rd Ⓖ good

PLASTIQUE KINETIC WORMS
A contemporary art space organised and managed by artists

The place to pick up contemporary artworks

Soobin Art Gallery (3, C5)

This terrific gallery introduced Singapore to China's boisterous avant-garde scene. It represents contemporary artists working in a range of styles, from the photorealism of Ai Xuan to Fang Lijun's pop art and Zhu Qizhan's traditional brush painting.

☎ 6837 2777 ☐ www.soo binart.com.sg ✉ 01-10/11/12 MICA Bldg, 140 Hill St ⏰ 11am-7pm Mon-Sat ⓂClarke Quay ♿ fair

Substation Gallery (3, C5)

This hip young gallery is part of the Substation arts complex, housed inside a renovated power station. Challenging, explorative and emotionally charged installations by up-and-coming

Get a buzz at the Substation

artists are the name of the game.

☎ 6337 7535 ☐ www.sub station.org ✉ 45 Armenian St ⏰ 11am-9pm Ⓜ City Hall ♿ fair

Utterly Art (5, C1)

Featuring mostly Singaporean painters and the odd photographer, this small, quality gallery on the fringes of Chinatown hosts regular exhibitions of contemporary work by locals such as Desmond Sim.

☎ 6226 2605 ☐ www .biotechnics.org/2utterlyart .html ✉ 02-01, 208 South Bridge Rd ⏰ 1.30am-8pm Mon-Sat, noon-5.30pm Sun Ⓜ Chinatown

STREET SCULPTURE

Singapore is dappled with a healthy crop of public sculpture by acclaimed local and international artists. Check out these babies:

- *Abundance* (3, E5) by Sun Yu Li – Suntec City
- *Between Sea & Sky* (3, E5) by Olivier Strehelle – Marina Mandarin Hotel, 6 Raffles Blvd
- *Bird* (3, D7) by Fernando Botero – UOB Plaza, Boat Quay
- *Homage to Newton* (3, D7) by Salvador Dali – UOB Plaza, Boat Quay
- *LOVE* (3, C4) by Robert Indiana – Penang Rd (above)
- *Milennium* (3, D6) by Victor Tan – Empress Place
- *Reclining Figures* (3, C7) by Henry Moore – OCBC Building
- *Seed* sculptures (3, E6) by Singaporean artist Han Sai Por – Esplanade waterfront garden
- *Six Brushstrokes* (3, E5) by Roy Lichtenstein – Millenia Walk, 9 Raffles Blvd

PLACES OF WORSHIP

See also Thian Hock Keng Temple (p15) and Sri Mariamman Temple (p17). Remove your shoes when entering temples, respect those at prayer and be prepared to cover your head at mosques. Entry to mosques is not permitted during prayer time.

Leong San See (Dragon Mountain) Temple

Armenian Church (3, C5)
Designed by colonial architect GD Coleman, the neoclassical Armenian Church of St Gregory the Illuminator is Singapore's oldest Christian church (1835). Pushing up orchids in the graveyard is Agnes Joaquim, discoverer of Singapore's national flower (Vanda Miss Joaquim orchid).
☎ 6334 0141 ✉ 60 Hill St ☼ 9am-5pm Mon-Fri, 9am-noon Sat, services Sun Ⓜ City Hall

Kong Meng San Phor Kark See Monastery (2, E3)
'Don't speak unless it improves the silence' at this astounding complex of dragon-topped pagodas, shrines, plazas and lawns linked by Escher-like staircases. The Pagoda of 10,000 Buddhas' golden stupa is lined with 9999 Buddha images – the 10,000th is the big boy inside.
☎ 6849 5300 ▢ www.km spks.org ✉ 88 Bright Hill Rd ☼ 6am-9pm Ⓜ Bishan Park, then bus 410 (white plate, not green)

Kwan Im Thong Hood Cho Temple (3, D4)
Dedicated to Guan Yin, the much-loved goddess of mercy, this modern temple (1982) is one of Singapore's busiest. Flower sellers, fortune tellers and incense-wielding devotees swarm around the entry and the magnificent golden Buddha.
✉ 178 Waterloo St ☼ 6am-6.15pm Ⓜ Bugis ♿ fair

Leong San See (Dragon Mountain) Temple (3, E1)
Built in 1917 using traditional joinery and intricately carved ceiling beams, this gorgeous Taoist/Buddhist temple has an effervescent, happy atmosphere. The smiling Buddha welcomes you at the door; to promote good feng shui, walk around clockwise. The Thai-style Buddhist **Temple of 1000 Lights** is across the road.
☎ 6298 9371 ✉ 371 Race Course Rd ☼ 6am-6pm Ⓜ Farrer Park ♿ fair

Temple of 1000 Lights

FESTIVAL OF THE HUNGRY GHOSTS

Every August or September the gates of hell are flung open and hungry ghosts return to Earth to haunt their relatives who must appease them. This is a time for banquets, street opera, puppet shows and burning miniature paper effigies of mobile phones, business suits, cars, 'hell money', and anything else you think you might need in the afterlife. The main action is in Chinatown – front-row seats are reserved for ghostly guests.

Lian Shan Shuang Lin Monastery (2, F3)

This photogenic place is a little out of the way, but it's well worth the journey. The atmospheric interior soars up to red- and ochre-hued ceilings, thick beams stained with decades of incense smoke. When the rain drowns out the traffic's growl, you could be anywhere in time. From the MRT station, walk down Lorong 6 Toa Payoh.
☎ 6259 6924 ✉ 184E Jln Toa Payoh ⏰ 7am-5pm Ⓜ Toa Payoh ♿ good

St Andrew's Cathedral

St Andrew's Cathedral (3, D5)

On a vast tract of prime inner-city real estate, St Andrew's was completed in 1861, built in early English Gothic style using Indian slave labour generously supplied by the British Empire. Its blue-white sheen derives from a sticky paint of shell lime, egg white and sugar.
☎ 6337 6104 💻 www
.livingstreams.org.sg ✉ 11 St Andrew's Rd ⏰ English services 9am Mon, Wed, Fri & Sat, 8am Tue, 9.30am Thu, 7am, 8am, 5pm & 7.30pm Sun Ⓜ City Hall ♿ fair

Sri Srinivasa Perumal Temple

Sri Srinivasa Perumal Temple (3, E1)

Dating from 1855 this is one of Singapore's most important temples, with the annual Thaipusam procession (see p61) kicking off under the hypercoloured *gopuram* (tower). Inside is a statue of Vishnu (aka Perumal), his consorts Lakshmi and Andal, and his bird-mount Garuda.
☎ 6298 5771 ✉ 397 Serangoon Rd ⏰ 6.30am-noon & 6-9pm Ⓜ Farrer Park ♿ good

Sri Veeramakaliamman Temple (Kali the Courageous) (3, D2)

This Shaivite temple exalts Kali, mother of Ganesh and Murugan, consort of Shiva, and bloodthirsty warrior against evil. Kali is big in Bengal, home of the labourers who built this temple in 1881. Craftsmen recently repainted the figures along the upper walls in a cavalcade of bodacious colours.
☎ 6293 4634 ✉ 141 Serangoon Rd ⏰ 8am-noon & 5.30-8.30pm Ⓜ Little India

Sultan Mosque (3, E3)

Named after Raffles' buddy Sultan Hussein Shah, this awesome gold-domed mosque accommodates 5000 worshippers. The glaring-red digital clock in the main hall compromises the atmosphere a little, but at least everybody knows when to pray. There is no entry on Friday.
☎ 6293 4405 💻 mjdsultn@pacific.net.sg ✉ 3 Muscat St ⏰ 9am-1pm & 2-4pm Sat-Thu Ⓜ Bugis

The Sultan Mosque on Arab St

PARKS & GARDENS

See also Singapore Zoo & Night Safari (p12), Singapore Botanic Gardens (p14), Bukit Timah Nature Reserve (p19) and Mt Faber (p21).

Bukit Batok Nature Park (2, D3)

This steamy, 36-hectare jungle enclave was developed in 1988 around a muddy quarry lake of interminable depth. Pathways and jogging trails wind through fecund, dripping forest past lookout points, orange cliffs and a small WWII memorial.
☎ 1800 471 7300
💻 www.nparks.gov.sg
✉ cnr Bukit Batok East Ave 2 & Bukit Batok East Ave 6 💲 free ⏲ 7am-7pm
Ⓜ Bukit Batok, then bus 61, 185, 521 ♿ fair

Chinese & Japanese Gardens (2, C3)

Highlights of the 13-hectare Chinese Gardens are the 176-step pagoda and the contorted Chinese bonsai (the 300-year-old *Pemphis acidula* steals the show). Pre-wedding photo sessions

The sacred shrine of Sultan Iskandar Shah, Fort Canning Park

dominate weekends. At the time of writing, the Japanese Gardens were undergoing wholesale renovations.
☎ 6261 3632 💻 explore@juronggardens.com.sg ✉ 1 Chinese Garden Rd 💲 free ⏲ 6am-11pm Ⓜ Chinese Garden ♿ good

East Coast Park (2, G4)

A good one for families: take a shady stroll, hire bikes or inline skates and terrorise pedestrians on the pathways, take a dip in the soupy Strait of Singapore or chill out with a beer at a beachfront restaurant (p53). After dark the many ships moored offshore look like another city.
✉ East Coast Parkway 💲 free ⏲ 24hr 🚌 16, 36 ♿ good

Fort Canning Park (3, C5)

When Raffles rocked into Singapore and claimed it for the mother country, locals steered clear of Bukit Larangan (Forbidden Hill) out of respect for the sacred shrine of Sultan Iskandar Shah, ancient Singapura's last ruler. Today's park features a cemetery, the old *keramat* (shrine) and the Battle Box museum (p22).
☎ 1800 471 7300 💻 www.nparks.gov.sg ✉ Cox Tce 💲 free ⏲ 24hr Ⓜ Dhoby Ghaut ♿ good

Jurong Birdpark (2, B4)

Built to give Singaporeans a dose of nature, Jurong is home to 8000 birds – 600 species, 30 of them endangered. Highlights include the Penguin Parade, the Waterfall Aviary, the nocturnal World of Darkness and various bird shows throughout the day. There's a 'panorail' ($4/2) to shunt you around if you're feeling lazy.
☎ 6265 0022 💻 www.birdpark.com.sg ✉ 2 Jurong Hill 💲 $14/7 ⏲ 9am-6pm Ⓜ Boon Lay, then bus 194, 251 ♿ good

MacRitchie Reservoir (2, E3)

A mirror-surfaced vision of tranquillity, MacRitchie

Sketching up a storm at the Chinese & Japanese Gardens

Reservoir is surrounded by a 12km, four-hour, circular jungle trail with a tree-top walkway (9am to 5pm Tuesday to Friday, 8.30am to 5pm Saturday and Sunday). The trail is organised into six colour-coded sectors – pick up a map at the rangers' office. You can also hire a kayak or go fishing.
☎ 6256 4248 🖳 www .nparks.gov.sg ✉ Lornie Rd 💲 free ⏱ 24hr Ⓜ Toa Payoh, then bus 157

National Orchid Garden (2, E4)
Nestled in the Singapore Botanic Gardens, the NOG's collection – an undeniably impressive 1000 species and 2000 hybrids – fills an orchidarium, cool room and mist house, amongst a plethora of water features.
☎ 6471 7361 🖳 www.sbg .org.sg ✉ Singapore Botanic Gardens, 1 Cluny Rd 💲 $5/1

'Singapore Sling anyone?' 'Pi pi pi pi'

FREEDOM OF SPEECH! WELL, ALMOST...

When **Speakers' Corner** (3, C6) was established in Hong Lim Park in 2000, it was seen as a victory for Singaporean democracy and freedom of speech. In the first month 400 speakers addressed enthusiastic crowds, but a year later only 11 braved the imposed restrictions. Anyone (except non-Singaporeans) can speak their mind, providing they register in advance with local police, avoid black-listed subjects (religion, politics, ethnicity), and don't violate Singapore's notorious sedition laws. These days Speakers' Corner is more like a whispering gallery. Shhhh...

⏱ 8.30am-7pm 🚌 7, 105, 123, 174, 502 ♿ good

Padang (3, D6)
Ringed by imposing colonial façades, there are few more obvious symbols of British imperialism than the Padang's manicured lawns. Defying the tropical heat, the Singapore Cricket Club (established 1852) struts its stuff to choruses of 'Huzzah!' and 'Cracking shot old bean!' from the members' pavilion. Rugby, bowls and football get an airing during the off-season. Cricket season is from February to September.
☎ 6471 9955 🖳 www.scc .org.sg ✉ Connaught Dr 💲 free ⏱ 24hr Ⓜ City Hall ♿ good

'Smashing shot!', Padang

Sungei Buloh Wetland Reserve (2, C1)
Attention bird-nerds! This 87-hectare park sustains 140 bird species and features mangrove boardwalks, walking trails, observation huts and guided tours on Saturday (9am, 10pm, 3pm and 4pm). It's a sweaty 20-minute hike from the Kranji Reservoir bus stop during the week – splurge on a cab from Kranji. On Sunday the bus stops at the park entrance.
☎ 6794 1401 🖳 www.sb wr.org.sg ✉ 301 Neo Tiew Cres 💲 $1/50¢ ⏱ 7.30am-7pm Mon-Sat, 7am-7pm Sun Ⓜ Kranji, then bus 925 ♿ fair

QUIRKY SINGAPORE

Fountain of Wealth (3, E5)

With a 30m water jet and 85 tonnes of excellent feng shui, the world's largest fountain isn't necessarily the world's most attractive. Between 8pm and 9pm you can project an 18m personalised laser message onto the water curtain.

☎ 6295 2888 ☐ www.sun teccity.com.sg ✉ Suntec City, 5 Temasek Blvd $ free ☼ 9am-10pm Ⓜ City Hall 🚌 10, 14, 70, 196, 547 ♿ good

Haw Par Villa: Tiger Balm Gardens (2, D4)

'That which is derived from society should be returned to society'. So said Aw Boon Haw, heir to the Tiger Balm fortune. What he returned

Haw Par Villa…subtle…No?

MEDICAL TOURISM

Fancy some cosmetic dentistry, angioplasty or perhaps a quick breast augmentation to really make your holiday memorable? Thailand and India are leading the pan-Asian boom in medical tourism, but Singapore isn't far behind. With affordable costs (10 times cheaper than the US), high-standard facilities and top-notch doctors, it's no wonder Westerners are queuing up for surgery after a morning shopping spree on Orchard Rd. And then there's your five-star hotel to recover in – after a few laps of the pool, your new hip will feel as good as new. Curious? Contact the **Singapore Tourism Board** (STB; ☎ 1800 736 2000; www.visitsingapore.com) for advice or check out www.singaporemedicine.com.

was an enormous concrete omelette enveloping the unbelievably kitsch Ten Courts of Hell, where grotesque Chinese statues depict sinners' fates in gory detail.

☎ 6872 2780 ☐ www .visitsingapore.com ✉ 262 Pasir Panjang Rd $ $1/50¢ ☼ 9am-7pm Ⓜ Buona Vista, then bus 200 ♿ good

Opera Karaoke (5, B2)

If you fancy yourself as a Chinese opera star (and who doesn't?), get your tonsils over to the Chinese Theatre Circle. Croon to your favourite opera hits, or enjoy the earnest vocal stylings of middle-aged businessmen. Giggling is not allowed.

☎ 6323 4862 ☐ www.ctco pera.com.sg ✉ 5 Smith St

$ incl tea & snacks $15 ☼ 2-5pm Tue-Sun Ⓜ Chinatown, Outram Park ♿ fair

Sky Dining (2, E5)

Impress the pants off the object of your affection with a romantic three-course dinner and sweeping views, while swinging 70m above Singapore in a glass-bottomed cable car. An interesting spot to get steamy; a bad place to break up. Book two working days in advance.

☎ 6277 9633 ☐ www .mountfaber.com.sg ✉ 109 Mt Faber Rd $ $88-158 ☼ 6.30-8.30pm Ⓜ HarbourFront, then cable car 🚌 shuttle from HarbourFront bus terminal (6pm-3am Mon-Fri, 7am-3am Sat & Sun)

SINGAPOREAN TV

Issues of media censorship aside, Singaporean TV provides an intriguing insight into the nation's social and ethnic demographics. Current affairs production credits start with 'Hair by…', while news bulletins lead with stories on Internet shopping trends (Middle-Eastern nuclear stand-offs are bumped down the list). Channel surf between B-grade Hollywood Westerns, cheesy local variety shows, slapstick Cantonese kung-fu soap operas, and around 40 years' worth of Bollywood musicals. Whatever you're watching, sex is a no-no but graphic violence is OK!

DAY SPAS

Singaporeans pride themselves on lookin' sharp. You'll never see anyone in shabby clothes, reflexology and massage are regulation indulgences, and everyone seems to have clear skin, clean nails and lustrously flowing hair. Check yourself into a day spa for an overhaul.

Amrita Spa (3, D5)
Super-swish international Amrita covers all the bases: massage, facials, body wraps, manicures, pedicures, waxing, and a suite of indulgent Ritual Packages (complete with disposable underwear). Their gym has all the requisite gadgets.
☎ 6336 4477 ☐ www.amritaspas.com ✉ 06-01 Raffles The Plaza, 80 Bras Basah Rd $ massages per 55min $105, facials $90-280, wraps $105-155, manicures/pedicures $40/45, waxing $25-80, packages $155-365, gym $63 ⏲ spa 10am-10pm, gym 5.30am-11pm Ⓜ City Hall

Kenko Wellness Spa (5, C1)
Kenko is the McDonalds of Singapore's spas with branches throughout the city, but there's nothing drive-through about its foot reflexology, romantic couples' sessions (per 2½ hour session $328) or Chinese and Swedish massage (Chinese is more forceful, using pointy elbows).
☎ 6223 0303 ☐ www.kenko.com.sg ✉ 199 South Bridge Rd $ reflexology per 30 min $33, massages per 30 min $49 ⏲ 10am-10pm Ⓜ Chinatown

Red Peach Boutique Spa (5, B1)
Peachy surrounds tempt you in the door here. Downstairs is a stylish interior-design gallery; upstairs you unwind in scented tatami booths as you wait for your body scrub, wax or aromatic facial. Ear candling will clear your jetlagged head.
☎ 6324 1250 ☐ spa@theredpeach.com ✉ 66/68 Pagoda St $ scrubs $68, waxing $25-70, facials $70-160, ear candling $58 ⏲ 11am-9pm Mon-Sat, noon-7.30pm Sun Ⓜ Chinatown

Snails the Nail Spa (4, C2)
Ponder your stock folio with Orchard Rd views at this sassy nail spa. Manicures and pedicures are sublime, while heiresses-in-waiting love the Little Princess deal ($15). Other treatments include the glamorous Dead & Fossilised ($65) and the submissive Geisha's Legendary ($55).
☎ 6738 0100 ✉ 03-01 Wheelock Pl, 501 Orchard Rd $ manicures/pedicures $25/35 ⏲ 10am-8pm Mon-Sat, 11am-6pm Sun Ⓜ Orchard

Gallery at Red Peach

Spa Esprit Downtown (4, D2)
This chic spa offers creative treatments in a retro setting; massage, facials, waxing and naturopathy are the staples. Boost your circulation with the blood-sucking Vampirella Wrap ($150), or vanquish 'cottage-cheese thighs' (their words, not ours) with the mechanised Endo Pump ($140).
☎ 6836 0500 ☐ www.spa-esprit.com ✉ 05-10 Paragon, 290 Orchard Rd $ massages per hr $95-165, facials $90-220, waxing $15-52 ⏲ 10am-9pm Mon-Sat, 10am-7pm Sun Ⓜ Orchard, Somerset

GET A HAIRCUT, AND GET A REAL JOB
Need a trim to beat the heat or want to turn your cut-and-colour into a 'lifestyle choice'? Try these on for size:
Frontiers Hairdressers (4, F2; ☎ 6235 2565; 01-12 Regency House, 123 Penang Rd; ⏲ 11am-8pm Mon-Sat, noon-6pm Sun; Ⓜ Somerset) A discreet retro-meets-Zen pod attracting fashion fans with chilled-out sounds, good coffee, aerodynamic barber chairs and chic shears by Hikiri and Jayson Lim.
Sabun Cabane (4, A3; ☎ 6235 2910; 03-22 Tanglin Mall, 163 Tanglin Rd; ⏲ 10am-7pm; Ⓜ Orchard) A kooky salon/gallery featuring modernist furnishings, floor-to-ceiling mirrors, groovy lighting, jazz, experimental cuts and glasses of red.

SINGAPORE FOR CHILDREN

With its clean, safe streets and family-centric values, Singapore is cool for kids (just ask all the pram-pushing expats). Children under 90cm tall ride free on the MRT and often receive admission discounts. See also Sentosa Island (p20), Singapore Zoo & Night Safari (p12) and Jurong Birdpark (p28).

Look for ⚐ listed with individual reviews in the Eating, Entertainment and Sleeping chapters for kid-friendly options.

Duck Tour (3, E5)
Take the kids on a one-hour Singapore tour in the Wacky Duck, a Vietnam War amphibious curio – half boat, half truck. Check out the city's sites from the road then hit the water for a harbour cruise. Beware the dire commentary.
☎ 6338 6877 🖳 www.duck tours.com.sg ✉ Suntec City, 5 Temasek Blvd 💲 $33/17 🕑 10am-6pm Ⓜ City Hall 🚌 10, 14, 70, 196, 547

Gymboree Play & Music (4, A3)
Designed for under-fives, Gymboree's classes focus on identifying if your kid is a 'logical thinker', 'emerging creative' or 'thoughtful observer'. Or maybe they just like drooling and bumping into things. Either way, they'll be out of your hair for a couple of hours.
☎ 6735 5290 🖳 gymbo ree@singnet.com.sg ✉ 03-17/18 Tanglin Mall, 163 Tanglin Rd 💲 per 2-hr class $30 🕑 9.30am-7pm Ⓜ Orchard

Jurong Reptile Park (2, C4)
It's a little run-down and probably not much fun for the crocodiles (they also appear on the park restaurant's menu), but kids get a kick out of watching the croc-wrestling (complete with heads-in-jaws), giant tortoises, Komodo dragons and pythons.
☎ 6261 8866 🖳 www.rep tilepark.com.sg ✉ 241 Jln Ahmad Ibrahim 💲 $8/7.50 🕑 9am-6pm, reptile show 11.45am & 2pm, croc feeding 10.30am & 5pm Ⓜ Boon Lay, then bus 194, 251 ♿ fair

'Awww-some!'

Orchard Skate Park & National Youth Centre (4, E3)
There's all kinds of stuff for big kids here: live outdoor bands, BMX displays, a graffiti wall, breakdance classes and a new skate park on Penang Rd. Fuel-up on banana fritters on Somerset Alley behind the centre.
☎ 6734 4233 🖳 www .youthopia.org.sg ✉ 113 Somerset Rd 💲 free 🕑 youth centre 9am-6pm Mon-Fri, noon-6pm Sat, skate park 7am-11pm Ⓜ Somerset ♿ good

Singapore Science Centre (2, C3)
The endearingly geeky Science Centre attracts kids like flies (plus a few adults pretending they're not interested). It's chock-full of exhibits, with regular demonstrations and plenty of push/pull/twist-and-see-what-happens action. The five-storey Omni-Theatre (p64) and Snow City (p33) are next door – an epic day out!
☎ 6425 2500 🖳 www .science.edu.sg ✉ 15 Science Centre Rd 💲 $6/3 🕑 10am-6pm Sat-Thu,

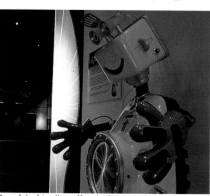
One of the friendly staff at the Singapore Science Centre

BABYSITTING

The **YMCA Metropolitan** (4, C1; ☎ 6839 8333; www .ymca.sg; 60 Stevens Rd) operates a crèche open to the children of the world for $25 per day. Alternatively, ask your hotel to organise a babysitter for you – they'll quite often allocate an experienced kid-proof member of staff to the task.

10am-9pm Fri Ⓜ Jurong East 🚍 66, 178, 198, 335 ♿ good

Snow City (2, C3)

If they're wilting in the heat, refrigerate the kids with a few well-aimed snowballs. It'll seem pretty lame if you're from anywhere cold, but the 60m toboggan slope regularly blows Singaporean minds. Admission includes jackets, boots and snow-tubes – bring socks, and call ahead for session times. ☎ 6560 2306 🖳 www .snowcity.com.sg ✉ 21 Jurong Town Hall Rd 💲 1-/2-hr session $12/18 ⏱ 10.30am-6.30pm Tue-Sun Ⓜ Jurong East 🚍 66, 178, 198, 335

Underwater World (1, A1)

Sentosa's saving grace, Gracie the dugong is Underwater World's star performer. Leafy sea-dragons and wobbling Medusa jellyfish are mesmeric; stingrays and 10ft sharks cruise overhead in the Ocean Colony's submerged glass tubes. Entry includes admission to the Dolphin Lagoon (shows 11am, 1.30pm, 3.30pm, 5.30pm) at Palawan Beach. ☎ 6275 0030 🖳 www .underwaterworld.com.sg ✉ 80 Siloso Rd, Sentosa Island 💲 $19.50/12.50 ⏱ 9am-9pm, Dolphin Lagoon 10.30am-6pm Ⓜ 🚍 see Sentosa Island p20 ♿ good

Wet Markets

The wet markets at **Chinatown Complex** (5, B2), **Tekka Centre** (3, D2) and **Geylang Serai Market** (2, G4) are squelchy, squishy, gross good fun, with baskets of stinky dried fish, squirming toads, stingrays, slippery eels…much more interesting than the supermarket! Watch your step – you don't want to end up sitting in the slime. It's best to go in the early morning. 💲 free

Wild Wild Wet (2, H3)

WWW is tons of watery fun – ride the four-storey speed slide, melt into the Jacuzzi, or kick back in a rubber tube and let the 'river' float you around the park. Don't forget sunscreen – the equatorial sun bites like a croc. ☎ 6581 9128 🖳 www .wildwildwet.com ✉ 1 Pasir Ris Close 💲 $12.90/8.80 ⏱ 9am-7pm Mon & Wed-Fri, 10am-7pm Sat & Sun Ⓜ Pasir Ris 🚍 3, 6, 21, 89, 354 ♿ good (pools only)

Check out your lunch options at Underwater World

TEEN SCENE

Singapore's mean streets are free from the blights of drugs, violence and rock 'n' roll, so parents can relax about letting the kids roam free. Hanging-out, munching junk food and looking cool whilst ogling members of the opposite sex is standard Orchard Rd practice – teen travellers will fit right in. Cinemas, pinball parlours and teen-friendly shops abound – check out Level One (p41), the Heeren (p41), and Orchard Skate Park & National Youth Centre (p32).

Tackle one of the Walking Tours below, or make friends with Singapore on your own terms. A wander along Orchard Rd (p9) is an elbows-out initiation, or ramble down North Bridge Rd, across the river and into Chinatown (p8), the city's cultural nucleus. Join the romantics for a night-time promenade along the Esplanade, or disorientate yourself in the colourful chaos of Little India (p10).

WALKING TOURS

Colonial Classic

From Raffles Place MRT, cut through the Clifford Centre shops and Change Alley overpass to historic **Clifford Pier** (**1**). Wander along the waterfront past the **One Fullerton Complex** (**2**), the **Merlion** (**3**; p22) and the **Fullerton Hotel** (**4**; p71). Beyond the iron arches of Anderson Bridge is the **Dalhousie Obelisk** (**5**), named after India's one-time governor-general. A statue of **Sir Stamford Raffles** (**6**) stands outside the decorous **Victoria Theatre & Concert Hall** (**7**). Dodge the Connaught Dr traffic and check out the **Lim Bo Seng Memorial** (**8**), honouring a WWII hero, the **Indian National Army Monument** (**9**) and the British **Cenotaph** (**10**). Take the Stamford Rd underpass to the **Civilian War Memorial** (**11**; p22), then head down St Andrew's Rd – catch some cricket at the **Padang** (**12**; p29) or a dose of piety at **St Andrew's Cathedral** (**13**; p27). South of here are the imposing **City Hall** (**14**), **Supreme Court** (**15**) and **Old Parliament House** (**16**). **Raffles Landing Site** (**17**; p22) is riverside – admire the main man before lunch at **IndoChine Waterfront** (**18**; p58). Afterwards, lose track of time at the **Asian Civilisations Museum** (**19**; p11) or cross Cavenagh Bridge for a boozy **Boat Quay** (**20**; p18) afternoon.

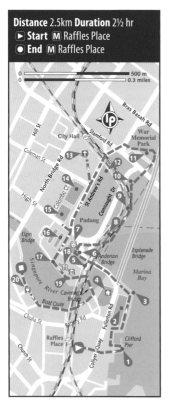

Distance 2.5km **Duration** 2½ hr
▶ **Start** Ⓜ Raffles Place
● **End** Ⓜ Raffles Place

Raffles – an imposing looking fellow

Rollin' On the River

Exiting Clarke Quay MRT, **Riverside Point** (**1**), formerly South Kampong Melaka, a swampy tidal village buzzing with trade, is upstream on the left. Pass the pragmatic trusses of **Ord Bridge** (**2**), named after the Straits Settlements' first governor, then duck under Clemenceau Bridge. The psychedelic **Alkaff Bridge** (**3**; p22) is named after a family of wealthy Arab settlers. Past the striking swoop of **Robertson Bridge** (**4**) is **Zouk** (**5**;

Gallery Hotel on Robertson Quay

p65), a hedonistic hub in the old Jiak Kim St godown (warehouses). Cross the improbably minimal **Jiak Kim Bridge** (**6**) to **Kim Seng Park** (**7**), named after a 1940s Chinese philanthropist, then cruise downstream along **Robertson Quay** (**8**), once thronging with boat repairers and timber mills. Near Saigon Bridge are the last of the river's **derelict godown** (**9**), held together with tree roots and rust – given Singapore's appetite for destruction, they won't last much longer! Continue downstream to **Bon Gout** (**10**; p58) for lunch. Check out the **Singapore Tyler Print Institute** (**11**; p24) then rummage through the restaurants and bars at **Clarke Quay** (**12**) (if you can stomach the architecture). Check out the galleries in the **MICA Building** (**13**; p24), visit the **Asian Civilisations Museum** (**14**; p11), or finish with a beer on **Circular Rd** (**15**; p18).

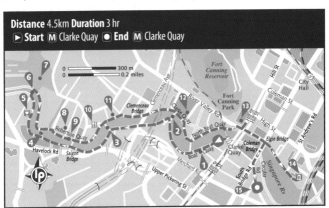

Distance 4.5km **Duration** 3 hr
▶ **Start** Ⓜ Clarke Quay ● **End** Ⓜ Clarke Quay

Arabic Amble

From Bugis MRT head southeast along Rochor Rd then swing left into North Bridge Rd to the high-gothic Art Deco fantasia of **Parkview Square** (**1**). Have a laugh with/at the **restaurant spruikers** (**2**) on the corner of Arab St, then duck down Haji Lane and catch a whiff of myrrh at **Kazura Perfumery** (**3**; ☎ 6293 1757; 51 Haji La). Continue to Beach Rd then turn left, and left again into Arab St, where overzealous fabric vendors and carpet salesmen abound. Slop up a hummus (creamy chickpea dip) lunch at **Café Le Caire** (**4**; p54), then veer right into Muscat St where the gold-topped **Sultan Mosque** (**5**; p27) shimmers. Trundle past renovated shophouses and palm trees on Bussorrah St, turn left into Baghdad St then left again into Sultan Gate for the **Malay Heritage Centre** (**6**; p22), historic seat of Malay royalty. Backtrack to Beach Rd and walk northeast to the **Hajjah Fatimah Mosque** (**7**) (aka the Leaning Tower of Singapore). Wiggle through onto Minto Rd, turn right onto Jln Sultan and continue to the **Malabar Muslim Jama-Ath Mosque** (**8**) on Victoria St. Overgrown with time and tree roots, the **Royal Cemetery** (**9**) is behind the mosque, its shambolic tombstones slowly succumbing to gravity. Boot it back down Victoria St to Bugis MRT to finish.

Malabar Muslim Jama-Ath Mosque

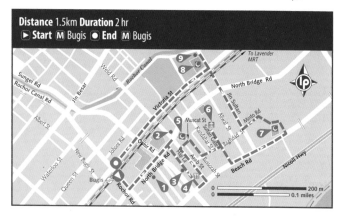

Distance 1.5km **Duration** 2 hr
▶ **Start** Ⓜ Bugis ⬤ **End** Ⓜ Bugis

DAY TRIPS
Pulau Bintan & Pulau Batam (6, C3 & D3)

Indonesia is a quick-fire ferry ride away, the islands of Bintan and Batam offering some psychological respite from Singapore's urbanity.

Bintan's main lures are the white-sand beaches and budget chalets on the **east coast**; luxury beach resorts and golf courses along the **north coast**; the endearing old port town **Tanjung Pinang**; and the ruins on nearby **Pulau Penyenget**. Bintan's resorts have little that's authentically Indonesian about them (other than the staff), but they're great stress-free getaways. Tanjung Pinang's stilt houses jut out over the water while, 200 years ago, Pulau Penyenget was an Islamic epicentre, the Riau-Lingga Kingdom holding sway from Java to Melaka.

Various operators run day trips to Bintan and Tanjung Pinang (you don't even have to change your Singapore dollars into rupiah!), but stay overnight to get the most from the island.

Batam has suffered rampant development since it was declared a free-trade zone in 1989, through-traffic nurturing a culture of exploitation, transience and sleaze. Things have improved recently though – gambling dens that drew Singaporean men like flies have closed down, while top-notch **spas** have been pulling in thousands of Singaporean ladies. The massive new **Waterfront City** development near the Sekupang ferry terminal fosters a family vibe, with cable skiing, go-karting and bowling. The northeastern Nongsa peninsula is ringed with verdant **golf resorts** built with Singaporean putters in mind.

INFORMATION

Bintan 45km, 1 hr from Singapore; Batam 20km, 40 min from Singapore

- 🚤 Bintan from Tanah Merah ferry terminal (2, J4), Batam from HarbourFront ferry terminal (1, B1)
- ☎ Bintan Resort Ferries 6542 4369, Batam Fast Ferries 6270 2228
- 🖳 www.bintan-resorts.com, www.visitsingapore.com
- 💲 Bintan return ferry $38-48, Batam $30-34
- 🕑 Bintan ferries 9am-8pm, Batam 7.30am-8pm
- ℹ Singapore Tourism Board (STB; ☎ 1800 736 2000; www.visit singapore.com)
- 🍴 resort and street restaurants

ISLANDS IN THE STREAM

Floating about 5km south of Singapore, **St John's Island** (2, E6) and **Kusu Island** (2, F6) make quiet beachy escapes with safe (if a little soupy) swimming. Culinary offerings are scant – pack a picnic. Check out Kusu's turtle sanctuary, Tua Pek Kong Chinese temple and the Malay Keramat Kusu shrine. **Ferries** (return $11/8; 🕑 10am & 1.30pm Mon-Sat, every 2 hr 9am-5pm Sun) depart Sentosa Ferry Terminal for Kusu (30 minutes) and St John's (45 minutes). Hire a bumboat from Clifford Pier (per hour around $100) to **Sisters' Islands** (2, E6) and **Lazarus Island** (2, F6), both unspoiled with super swimming, snorkelling and diving. BYO food and drinks.

Pulau Ubin (2, H2)

A chugging, smoky bumboat ride from Changi Point Ferry Terminal lands you on Pulau Ubin's shores. Singaporeans wax nostalgic about the island's *kampung* (village) atmosphere, but it's only a matter of time before Ubin strays into the developers' sights. For the moment though, it remains a lazily unkempt expanse of jungle, full of fast lizards, weird shrines and cacophonic birdlife. Battered taxis wait by the pier while drivers chew the fat, chickens squawk and panting dogs slump in the dust.

INFORMATION

10 min by bumboat from Changi Point ferry terminal

- Ⓜ Tanah Merah, then bus 2 to Changi village, bumboat to Palau Ubin
- ☎ information kiosk 6542 4108
- 🖳 www.nparks.gov.sg
- $ bumboat $2 one-way
- ☯ bumboats 6am-8pm
- ⓘ information kiosk 8.30am-5pm
- ✗ eateries near ferry terminal

The best way to get around is by **mountain bike**, costing $5 to $10 a day, which, coincidentally, is also about the only thing to do – the tidal mud flats are lousy for swimming and the enticingly blue quarry lakes are off limits.

Feeling energetic?

Veer right from the jetty to the information kiosk: pick up a half-decent map and sniff around the exhibition on Ubin's culture, history and wildlife. You can also take a guided trip to the **Tanjong Chek Jawa** mangrove swamps in the island's east from here (tours per group around $60); call the information kiosk, or consult the website for dates. Alternatively, just trundle off on your bike and see where the road takes you.

There are plenty of places to eat near the ferry terminal – complete your island adventure with some chilli crab and Tiger beer as the Bee Gees wail shamelessly from the stereo.

PULAU TIOMAN

Need a break? Hop on a **Berjaya Air** (☎ 6227 3688; www.berjaya-air.com) flight to the Malaysian island of Tioman. High peaks, dense jungle and beautiful beaches with excellent snorkelling and diving await. There's a bottomless bucket of accommodation here, most of which are basic wooden beach chalets with bed, fan and bathroom. The main villages are Salang, Juara, Tekek and Air Batang (usually called ABC); Salang has the best nightlife and proximity to Monkey Bay and Pulau Tulai dive sites. Flights depart Singapore's Seletar Airport (2, F2) at 1.55pm daily, costing around $280 return.

ORGANISED TOURS

The **Singapore Tourism Board** (STB; ☎ 1800 736 2000; www.visitsingapore .com) books tours and publishes a handful of free self-guided walking tour brochures. The SIA Hop-On, CityBuzz and Singapore Trolley buses (p84) traverse Singapore's most-loved sites, or tackle the amphibious Duck Tour (p32). Travel agents throughout the city offer competitive package tours to Malaysia and Indonesia.

Cheng Ho Harbour Cruise (3, D7)
The Cheng Ho is a big ol' oriental bucket floating around the harbour, port and Kusu Island on morning- and afternoon-tea cruises. Their dinner cruise loops past Sentosa. ☎ 6533 9811 ☐ www.watertours.com.sg ✉ 01-31 Clifford Pier $ 2½-hr morning cruise $25/12, afternoon $29/14, 2-hr dinner cruise $53/27 Ⓜ Raffles Place ☾ 10.30am, 3pm & 6.30pm

Eastwind Harbour Cruises (3, D7)
Eastwind's Chinese junk recently burned to the seafloor, but their other boats still do daytime and evening cruises around the waterfront and islands (Kusu, Lazarus, St John's, Sisters' and Sentosa). ☎ 6533 3432 ☐ www.fairwind.com.sg ✉ 01-30A Clifford Pier $ 40-min cruise $22/15, 2½-hr cruise with buffet dinner $36/18 Ⓜ Raffles Place ☾ hourly; dinner cruise 6pm

COOKING UP A STORM
If you learn how to cook Singapore-style you won't need to come back! Classes run from two to four hours; some are hands-on, some are instruction only. Call for bookings and schedules.

at-sunrice (3, C5; ☎ 6336 3307; www.at-sunrice .com; Fort Canning Centre, Fort Canning Park; classes $75-100; Ⓜ Dhoby Ghaut) Half-day classes with a spicy hands-on emphasis.

Cookery Magic (2, G4; ☎ 6348 9667; www.cookery magic.com; Haig Rd, Katong; classes $50-60; Ⓜ Paya Lebar) Ruqxana's classes for beginners in her own home.

Coriander Leaf (3, C6; ☎ 6732 3354; www.coriander leaf.com; 02-03 Clarke Quay; classes from $110; Ⓜ Clarke Quay) Pan-Asian and Euro delights for small groups. See also p58.

Raffles Culinary Academy (3, D5; ☎ 6412 1256; www.raffleshotel.com; 02-17 Raffles Hotel, 1 Beach Rd; classes $65-130; Ⓜ City Hall) Chinese, Indian and Thai straight from Raffles' kitchens.

Shermay's Cooking School (2, E4; ☎ 6479 8442; www.shermay.com; 03-64 Block 43, Jln Merah Saga, Chip Bee Gardens, Holland Village; classes $50-60; ☒ 7, 61, 77) Singaporean, Peranakan and chocolate are Shermay's faves!

Singapore Explorer (3, C6)
These guys run glass-topped boat (air-conditioned) and bumboat (naturally breezy) cruises up and down the river. There's plenty to see – the commentary will ensure you know what you're looking at. ☎ 6339 6833 ☐ www .singaporeexplorer.com.sg ✉ Clarke Quay $ 45-min glass-topped boat cruise $16/8, 30-min bumboat cruise $13/7 Ⓜ Clarke Quay ☾ cruises at regular intervals 9am-11pm

Singapore River Cruise
Cruise beneath the bridges and bumble along the quays on a 'River Experience' bumboat, from the Merlion at the river-mouth upstream to Robertson Quay plus everything in between. ☎ 6336 6111 ☐ www .rivercruise.com.sg ✉ 9 jetties; call for closest location $ 30-45 min cruise $15/8 ☾ cruises at regular intervals 9am-11pm

Trishaws (3, D3)
Trishaw drivers work hard for their money. If you don't mind feeling like a colonial overlord, sit back and cruise through Little India and Chinatown on these nifty three-wheelers. ✉ cnr Waterloo & Albert Sts $ per 30 min $40-60 Ⓜ Bugis

Shopping

Shopping is locked in an age-old struggle with eating and movie-going for the title of Singapore's national hobby. Fuelled by a raging pyre of slick advertising, frenzied crowds throng through the doors of department stores and enormous malls across the city. This is hard-core capitalism – failure to participate is not an option!

Compared with Thailand, Indonesia and Malaysia, Singapore is no bargain-hunter's paradise, and prices are usually fixed except at markets and in tourist areas. A 5% GST tax refund on goods worth $300 or more can be applied for through shops participating in the Global Refund scheme (look for the 'Tax Free Shopping' logo). Pick up a *How to Shop Tax Free in Singapore* brochure at the airport or visitors centres.

Serious problems with retailers are unlikely (the worst you'll probably get is lethargic service), but if you've been ripped-off or taken for a ride, contact the **Singapore Tourism Board** (STB; ☎ 1800 736 2000; www.visitsingapore.com) or the **Small Claims Tribunal** (3, B6; ☎ 6435 5994; www.smallclaims .gov.sg; Subordinate Courts, 1 Havelock Sq; ☻ 8.30am-1pm & 2-5pm Mon-Fri, 8.30am-1pm Sat). Tourist complaints are usually heard within two or three days.

The STB-endorsed **Great Singapore Sale** storms through June and July every year – two months of discount shopping coinciding with various arts and food festivals. Check out www.greatsingaporesale .com.sg.

SHOPPING HOT SPOTS

Orchard Road is the traditional megamall drawcard, while small backstreet businesses in **Chinatown** (antiques, textiles, modern 'oriental' homeware, crappy T-shirts), **Little India** (saris, CDs, glass bracelets, carved furnishings, religious art, wall hangings) and **Kampong Glam** (fabrics, woven rattan mats, baskets, carpets, traditional perfumes and slyly muttering tailors – 'How 'bout a sweeeet suit sir?') offer less multinational experiences. Street markets aren't as big in Singapore as in most Asian cities, but you'll find everything from cheap bags to Che Guevara T-shirts and tattoo parlours at **Bugis Street Market** (3, D4; ☻ 10am-10pm).

LOCAL DESIGNERS & BOUTIQUES

Blackjack (4, E2)

Blackjack's designer men's threads are a fashion ace up your sleeve. Brands include Buddhist Punk and Fresh Jive, as well as Australian brands Vicious Threads, Mooks and Sass & Bide (for women), and the jeans maestro Tsubi.
☎ 6735 0975 ✉ 01-10 Forum Shopping Mall, 583 Orchard Rd ☯ 10.30am-7pm Mon-Sat, 11am-6pm Sun Ⓜ Orchard

Edge (3, E4)

Edge is a thicket of local streetwear outlets wedged into a corner of Parco Bugis Junction shopping centre. Businesses cut and run with frightening speed; enduring beyond the norm are Pure Milk (mildly subversive T-shirts), 77th Street (club wear with force-fed attitude) and Refugees (paramilitary rebellion).
☎ 6557 6557 ✉ 03 Parco Bugis Junction, 200 Victoria St ☯ 11am-9pm Ⓜ Bugis

Heeren (4, E2)

On levels four and five of this teen-scene shopping mall, a labyrinth of anarchic designers flog home-grown creations and avant-garde rip-offs from microboutiques. Favourites include Groove Designs (guys' shirts), Ground Zero (bum-hugging denim shorts) and the intriguingly named Fourskin (for lads, of course!).
☎ 6733 4725 ✉ 260 Orchard Rd ☯ 10.30am-10pm Ⓜ Somerset

Level One (4, C1)

Teen-queens drag their sleepwalking boyfriends from shop to shop in this microboutique playground billing itself The Fashion Incubator. Amongst the costume jewellery, funky hairdressers and graffiti wall are some quality shops: keep an eye out for Future State (jeans and slinky tops) and the weird creations at Womb.
☎ 6235 2411 ✉ 01 Far East Plaza, 14 Scotts Rd ☯ 10am-10pm Ⓜ Orchard

M)phosis (4, D2)

M)phosis' Ngee Ann City branch (one of nine around town) stocks colour-coded miniature wisps of girly, slinky, sexy stuff; nice knits; and elegant pieces by local designer Colin Koh. You'll increase your chances of actually fitting into something if you buy two pieces and sew them together.
☎ 6737 6539 ✉ B1-09/10 Ngee Ann City, 391 Orchard Rd ☯ 10.30am-9.30pm Ⓜ Orchard, Somerset

POA People of Asia (3, E4)

Skate styles for the boys swerve dangerously close to office wear; I'm-cute-but-quirky girls' items fly off the shelves. Street press is piled high on the sales counter; 20-something sales assistants chew gum and rock-out to blaring in-store pop. People of Asia, this is your world!
☎ 6333 4582 ✉ 02-10 Parco Bugis Junction, 200 Victoria St ☯ 10.30am-9.30pm Ⓜ Bugis

Projectshop (4, D2)

Popular local streetwear label selling summery gear – tank tops, cutesy T-shirts and sun dresses for girls; cargo pants for boys – plus bags, belts and wallets at reasonable prices, with unpretentious service. Can't decide what to buy? Refocus your desires over coffee and cake at the **Projectshop Café** next door.
☎ 6735 0071 ✉ 03-41/44 Paragon, 290 Orchard Rd ☯ 10.30am-10pm Ⓜ Orchard, Somerset

SINGAPORE'S DESIGNERS

Singapore's shopping malls overflow with big-name international brands, but local designers can be just as fresh, sexy and offbeat as anyone! Keep an eagle-eye out for seductive black evening wear by Anthea Chan's label **Perfect In Black** (www.perfectinblack.com); elegant, well-cut after-five dresses by **Daniel Yam** (www.daniel yam.com); limited-edition offbeat sexy flash-fashion by Madeline Wong and Jay Quek's label **Posse** (☎ 9753 0692); distinctive, textured and layered kookiness from K Mi Huang's **Womb** (www.w-o-m-b.com); and flamboyant cocktail dresses and handmade accessories from rising star Beno Asmoro's label **Beno La Mode** (www .benolamode.com). Contact designers directly or check websites for outlets and availability.

INTERNATIONAL BRANDS

Birkenstock (4, A3)

Birkenstock has cornered the market in comfortable sandals, their Singapore shop stocking a flamboyant range of styles and sizes (including kids' sizes), ideally worn with socks. A million German backpackers can't be wrong! ☎ 6835 2702 ✉ 02-27 Tanglin Mall, 163 Tanglin Rd ⏱ 11am-8.45pm Ⓜ Orchard ⊞ 7, 77, 106, 111, 174

Etro (4, D2)

Locked in a love-hate relationship with fashion police, Etro pits plaid against paisley, clashes corduroy with cow-hide and hangs stripy shirts over suede bowling shoes. The results are entirely interesting. You might look like a freak, but no-one will say you're thin on individuality. ☎ 6737 5108 ✉ 01-30 Paragon, 290 Orchard Rd ⏱ 10.30am-8.30pm Ⓜ Orchard, Somerset

Will my chihuahua fit in that?

Jean-Paul Gaultier (4, D2)

JPG's boudoir-inspired boutique was designed by Philippe Starck and features silk-padded dressing rooms, cut-crystal clothes racks and sales assistants in trademark blue-and-white stripy T-shirts. ☎ 6733 4403 ✉ 01-03 Paragon, 290 Orchard Rd ⏱ 10am-9pm Ⓜ Orchard, Somerset

Levi's (3, D5)

Despite the humidity's clammy grip, jeans are *de rigueur* in Singapore. Legendary Levi's have re-invented themselves for the Asian market with more than a dozen shops around town. Rigid, engineered, scarred, loose, straight or flared – 'What's your story?' ☎ 6334 5501 ✉ 01-32 Raffles City, cnr Stamford & North Bridge Rds ⏱ 10am-10pm Ⓜ City Hall

Louis Vuitton (4, D2)

Check out the window display! (As if you could miss it.) Inside, badly dressed IT geeks and business moguls sweat quietly on couches while their wives pick out something gorgeous. Life-size catwalk models flit past on big screens while the doorman tries not to watch. Prices aren't labelled – if you have to ask, you probably can't afford it. ☎ 6734 7760 ✉ 01 Takashimaya, Ngee Ann City, 391 Orchard Rd ⏱ 10.30am-9pm Ⓜ Orchard, Somerset

CLOTHING & SHOE SIZES

Women's Clothing

Aust/UK	8	10	12	14	16	18
Europe	36	38	40	42	44	46
Japan	5	7	9	11	13	15
USA	6	8	10	12	14	16

Women's Shoes

Aust/USA	5	6	7	8	9	10
Europe	35	36	37	38	39	40
France only	35	36	38	39	40	42
Japan	22	23	24	25	26	27
UK	3½	4½	5½	6½	7½	8½

Measurements approximate only; try before you buy.

Men's Clothing

Aust	92	96	100	104	108	112
Europe	46	48	50	52	54	56
Japan	S	M	M		L	
UK/USA	35	36	37	38	39	40

Men's Shirts (Collar Sizes)

Aust/Japan	38	39	40	41	42	43
Europe	38	39	40	41	42	43
UK/USA	15	15½	16	16½	17	17½

Men's Shoes

Aust/UK	7	8	9	10	11	12
Europe	41	42	43	44½	46	47
Japan	26	27	27.5	28	29	30
USA	7½	8½	9½	10½	11½	12½

Muji (3, E4)

Shopping for shopping's sake, everything at Muji is small, neatly packaged and very Japanese. Stock up on teensy colour-coordinated travel, household and stationery items, wardrobe basics, storage systems and other stuff you don't really need.

☎ 6273 8833 ✉ 02 Seiyu Department Store, Parco Bugis Junction, 200 Victoria St ⏱ 10.30am-10pm Mon-Fri, 10am-10pm Sat & Sun Ⓜ Bugis

Prada (4, D2)

Prada turns the act of carrying something from A to B into a sensuous art form. Shoes, wallets, key-rings, perfume and gloves compliment their bags with lashings of Milano flair. Oh, and the clothes aren't bad either (especially if you're spending someone else's money).

☎ 6735 5715 ✉ 01-45/46 Paragon, 290 Orchard Rd ⏱ 10am-9pm Ⓜ Orchard, Somerset

Stussy (4, C2)

Stussy stocks skate, surf and streetwear for shaggy teens and adults who aren't quite ready to bid the beach goodbye. Surfy co-conspirators **f** hang out in the same complex.

☎ 6738 2270 ✉ 01-07/08 Pacific Plaza, 9 Scotts Rd ⏱ 11am-8.30pm Mon-Sat, 11am-7.30pm Sun Ⓜ Orchard

Versace (4, D2)

Shoes, jeans and catwalk screens – Versace shines with fashion riches. Skinny service staff are appropriately louche, oblique and Mediterranean

BAG LADY

Salivating handbag fetishists can send themselves to leather heaven on Level 3 of the **DFS Galleria** (4, C1; 25 Scotts Rd) and at **Paragon** (4, D2; 290 Orchard Rd): Louis Vuitton, Fendi, Gucci, Salvatore Ferragamo, Burberry, Dior, Prada, Coach, Valentino, YSL, Loewe… Bag yourself a bargain, or beat your credit card into submission.

Prada pumps

(there's no effusiveness here – it would ruin the mystique).

☎ 6738 5028 ✉ 01-04/05 Paragon, 290 Orchard Rd ⏱ 10.30am-9pm Ⓜ Orchard, Somerset

Zara (4, D2)

Fashionistas get more for less at this Spanish chain selling affordable, fashionable clothes, designs resembling the originals as soon as they've mooched off the catwalk. Racks of suits, shoes and stylin' informal gear are replenished from Europe every two weeks.

☎ 6735 1018 ✉ B1-15/24, Ngee Ann City, 391 Orchard Rd ⏱ 10am-9.30pm Ⓜ Orchard, Somerset

Something to (nearly) wear at Louis Vuitton

FOOD & DRINK

In addition to the speciality stores below, don't miss the wet markets at the **Chinatown Complex** (5, B2), **Tekka Centre** (3, D2) and **Geylang Serai Market** (2, G4) for a dose of the fundamentals. Local supermarket chains **Carrefour** and **Cold Storage** have branches in most major shopping malls and also sell booze.

Bees Brand Birds Nest (5, B1)

Here's where you can stock up on everything to please the fussiest of guests: chocolate bubble-tea mix, wild ginseng and whole (or grated) saiga antelope horn. And you can never have too many XL dried sea cucumbers in the larder. ☎ 6224 5691 ✉ 64 Smith St ⏱ 10am-9pm Ⓜ Chinatown

Khan Mohamed Mhoy & Sons (3, D2)

Follow your nose to what may be the last traditional spice-grinding shop in Singapore. Plastic garbage bins full of dried bell chillies crowd the doorway, while inside you can take away big scoops of turmeric, cumin and fennel or order them freshly ground. ☎ 6293 6191 ✉ 20 Cuff Rd ⏱ 8am-8.30pm Ⓜ Little India

Komala Vilas Sweet Shop (3, D2)

Hypercoloured North- and South-Indian sweets glisten luridly on trays, with enough shimmers of edible silver and gold foil to rival a Bollywood bride's spangles. Orange,

Komala Vilas Sweet Shop

green and yellow; sticky, shiny and gelatinous – take them away by the bag-full. ☎ 6294 3294 ✉ 82 Serangoon Rd ⏱ 11am-9.30pm Ⓜ Little India

Lazy Gourmet Deli by Les Amis (4, C2)

Sandwiched (ha! ha!) between the two Les Amis restaurants, Lazy Gourmet has everything you need for a DIY French picnic: pralines from Lyon, tins of duck fat, mini jars of *cassoulet* (white bean, meat and vegetable casserole) and *cornichons* (pickled baby cucumbers),

breads, pastries and vegetables. Businessmen browse the vacuum-packed stews for lonely TV dinners. ☎ 6333 8722 ✉ 02-10 Shaw Centre, 1 Scotts Rd ⏱ 10.30am-8.30pm Mon-Fri, 10.30am-9.30pm Sat & Sun Ⓜ Orchard

Supernature (4, B3)

Supernature is Singapore's best organic deli, their shelves heaving with chemical- and gluten-free veggies, groceries, baby food, wine and meats. They also do a roaring trade in organic coffee and take-away juices (try the predictably green 'Incredible Hulk'). ☎ 6735 4338 ✉ 01-21 Park House, 21 Orchard Blvd ⏱ 10am-7pm Mon, Tue, Thu & Sat, 10am-8pm Wed & Fri, 11am-6pm Sun Ⓜ Orchard

KIDS 'R' US

Singapore's kids and teens are commercially catered for by a gaggle of clothes and toy shops. Here are some of the best:

Bugis Street Market (3, D4; ⏱ 10am-10pm) Heavy metal T-shirts and low-grade rebellion.

Forum Shopping Mall (4, B2; 583 Orchard Rd; ⏱ 10am-10pm) Kid-sized DKNY, Ralph Lauren, Guess and Benetton gear.

Heeren (4, E2) Another spot for teens; see p41.

Kinokuniya (4, D2) Kids' books by the truckload; see p46.

Level One (4, C1) Good for teens; see p41.

Mothercare (3, E5; ☎ 6513 3212; 02-03 Suntec City; ⏱ 11.30am-9pm) For all your bootie and mollycoddling requirements.

Robinsons (3, D5; ☎ 6216 8388; 03-01 Raffles City; ⏱ 10.30am-9.30pm) A family-focussed department store.

Toys 'R' Us (4, B2; ☎ 6235 4322; 03-03/25 Forum Shopping Mall, 583 Orchard Rd; ⏱ 10am-10pm) A celebration of international toydom.

ARTS, CRAFTS, HOMEWARE & ANTIQUES

Dempsey Road (2, E4)
Populating the spooky former British army barracks along Dempsey Rd are warehouse-style outlets stocking everything from restored and reproduction Chinese antiques to Kashmiri carpets and Burmese Buddhist statues. There's even a wine bar to help while away the time.
✉ Dempsey Rd 🕙 11am-7pm 🚌 106, 123, 174

Lifestory (2, E4)
If you're here on holiday you probably won't want to buy a wardrobe, but Lifestory (and **White Collection** next door) provides an interesting insight into contemporary Singapore's domestic aspirations. Fashionable household ephemera and furnishings by international designers adorn bedroom installations and kitchen displays as R&B blings from speakers – very good looking; not very affordable.
☎ 6732 7362 ✉ 02-33D Great World City, 1 Kim Seng Promenade 🕙 11am-9pm 🚌 16, 75, 195, 970

Royal Selangor (3, C6)
On an island devoid of natural resources like gold and silver, pewter is the next best thing. Take a tour of Royal Selangor's pewter gallery (including pewtersmithing demo $2) then gawp at the shiny things in the retail cabinets. A dimpled hip flask will set you back $120; a beer mug $75.
☎ 6268 9600 ✉ 01-01 Clarke Quay 🕙 9am-9pm Ⓜ Clarke Quay

SINGAPORE MALL CRAWL

Singapore's shopping malls embody the prosperity and abundance so deeply craved by its citizens. The major malls open their doors around 10am, and stay open until the last moviegoers and food court–feasters go home around midnight. Commercially, things can be a bit hit-and-miss; here's a handful of hits:

Heeren (4, E2; 260 Orchard Rd) A massive HMV downstairs; a warren of local designer outlets on levels four and five; see also p41.

Ngee Ann City (4, D2; 391 Orchard Rd) The grandmama of them all, with Takashimaya department store, Kinokuniya, a vast food court and resident gods Cartier, Chanel and Louis Vuitton.

Paragon (4, D2; 290 Orchard Rd) Classy, classy, classy: Givenchy, Ralph Lauren, YSL, Hugo Boss, Versace, Gucci, Jean-Paul Gaultier, Prada et al.

Raffles City (3, D5; cnr Stamford & North Bridge Rds) Mainstream and city centre, business types heave between jeans shops and the food court.

Suntec City (3, E5; 3 Temasek Blvd) A gargantuan four-tier complex with cinemas, Tower Records, countless restaurants and the Fountain of Wealth (p30).

Tanglin Mall (4, A3; 163 Tanglin Rd) An expat heaven/haven with kids in prams, midrange boutiques and a pastel-hued food court.

Wheelock Place (4, C2; 501 Orchard Rd) The sanest mall of all, with Borders, quality restaurants and specialty stores.

Tanglin Shopping Centre (4, A2)
Level two of the Tanglin Shopping Centre (not to be confused with Tanglin Mall) is chock-full of cool art galleries and Singapore's best antiques shops. Carpets, wall hangings, artworks, cabinets and trinkets festoon the windows. Bargaining is expected.
☎ 6732 8751 ✉ 19 Tanglin Rd 🕙 10am-6pm Mon-Sat, 11am-4pm Sun Ⓜ Orchard

Zhen Lacquer Gallery (5, B1)
Generally kitsch but sometimes stylish, the shiny lacquered stuff at Zhen will at least keep your eyes entertained for a few minutes. Hand-painted jewellery boxes, placemat sets, utensils, plates and photo albums are the pick of the crop.
☎ 6222 2718 ✉ 1/1A/1B Trengganu St 🕙 9.30am-6.30pm Ⓜ Chinatown

MUSIC & BOOKS

Indian Classical Music Centre (3, D3)

This small shop has a supply of everything the aspiring Sergeant Pepper needs to slot into the Hindustani groove: sitar, tabla, bells – wearable and shakeable – and CDs to drown out your efforts.
☎ 6291 0187 ✉ 26 Clive St ⏱ 10am-8pm Mon-Sat, 10am-4pm Sun Ⓜ Little India

Kinokuniya (4, D2)

Brahms wafts across the head-high shelves at Kinokuniya, the biggest bookshop in Southeast Asia – you could get lost in here for days. There's a kids' reading area with books strewn across the floor, regional literature, a comics section and more Lonely Planet guides than we knew existed.
☎ 6737 5021 ✉ 03-09/15 Ngee Ann City, 391 Orchard Rd ⏱ 10.30am-9.30pm Sun-Fri, 10am-10pm Sat Ⓜ Orchard, Somerset

That CD Shop (4, C2)

Filling a two-storey warehouse with stacks of CDs, comfy leather couches, subtle downlights, free coffee and a Nakamichi sound system that sets the chandeliers

CHAIN GANGS

Mainstream chains dominate Singapore's music scene – try **HMV** (4, E2; ☎ 6733 1822; The Heeren, 260 Orchard Rd; ⏱ 10am-11pm), **Tower Records** (3, E5; ☎ 6338 0758; 02-63/67 Suntec City; ⏱ 10am-10pm), **Sembawang Music Centre** (4, E3; ☎ 6738 7727; 03-01 Cineleisure Orchard, Grange Rd; ⏱ 10am-11pm) and **Gramophone** (4, C2; ☎ 6235 2011; B1-27 Scotts Shopping Centre, 6 Scotts Rd; ⏱ 11am-9pm).

For books, try **MPH Bookstores** (3, E5; ☎ 6835 7637; B1-26A CityLink Mall; ⏱ 10am-9.30pm), or the ever-reliable **Borders** (4, C2; ☎ 6235 7146; 01-00 Wheelock Pl, 501 Orchard Rd; ⏱ 9am-11pm).

Kinokuniya on Orchard Rd

a-rockin', this feels less like consumerism and more like a party. Consider moving in on a permanent basis.
☎ 6238 6720 ✉ 01-01/02 Pacific Plaza, 9 Scotts Rd ⏱ 11am-midnight Ⓜ Orchard

V & V Music Centre (3, D3)

Indian and Bangladeshi expats swarm to V & V for the latest subcontinental

hits, sacred chants and Bollywood soundtracks. Mix 'em up for a musical extravaganza at home. Louder than love, **Jothi Music Centre** (3, D3; ☎ 6299 5528; 01-77 Campbell Block, Little India Arcade; ⏱ 10am-10pm) pumps sexy Indian dance music into the street.
☎ 6927 6467 ✉ 144 Dunlop St ⏱ 11am-10pm Ⓜ Little India

BOOKISH SINGAPORE

Singapore's most celebrated novels include *Tigers in Paradise* by Philip Jeyaretnam, *Juniper Loa* by Lin Yutang, *Tangerine* by Colin Cheong, *Playing Madame Mao* by Lau Siew Mai, and *Mammon Inc* by Tan Hwee Hwee. Short story fans should read *Little Ironies* by Catherine Lim and *12 Best Singapore Stories* by Goh Sin Tub. Poetry fiends might enjoy Landmark Books' *One Fierce Hour*. For politics try the hefty *Singapore Story: Memoirs of Lee Kuan Yew*, or *Singapore: The Air-Conditioned Nation* by Cherian George. *King Rat* by James Clavell will rattle war buffs, while speed-readers might attempt Time Books' *Culture Shock Singapore!* For architecture, see Robert Powell's *Singapore Architecture*.

SPECIALIST STORES

Bookbinders Design
(4, D2)
Thinking inside the box, this place has colourful Swedish-made notepaper, photo albums, chunky hard-backed travel journals, notebooks and plenty of substantial, sensible boxes to put them all in.
☎ 6737 0445 ⊠ 04-20 Ngee Ann City, 391 Orchard Rd ⏱ 10am-9pm Ⓜ Orchard, Somerset

Eu Yan Sang (5, C2)
Venerable Eu Yan Sang has been revamped to look like a Western chemist – but check out the traditional remedies on the shelves! Blood nourishment soaps, bird's nest six-packs, century eggs… A consultation with the herbalist costs $12; most remedies come with English instructions. Neighbouring **Teck Soon Medical Hall** (5, C2;
☎ 6227 6179; 281 South Bridge Rd; ⏱ 9am-6pm) trades in similar miracles.
☎ 6223 6333 ⊠ 269 South Bridge Rd ⏱ 9am-6pm Mon-Sat Ⓜ Chinatown

L'Occitane En Provence
(3, E5)
Stamp out free radicals and regenerate your face at this stellar French store. Shampoos, balms, soaps, moisturisers, oils and scented candles are laced with honey, lavender, citrus, almond and

ELECTRONICA
In Singapore you buy on one basis only – price. Hi-tech goods are just the same as you'd get back home, so quality doesn't enter into it. Most stores offer competitive duty-free prices, but haggle if there's a discrepancy between the shelf price and what the item is actually worth (do some homework). Hardwire yourself into six floors of big brands at **Funan Digital Life Mall** (3, D5; ☎ 6336 8327; 109 North Bridge Rd; ⏱ 10.30am-8.30pm) or the legendary **Sim Lim Square** (3, D3; ☎ 6338 3859; 1 Rochor Canal Rd; ⏱ 10.30am-9pm).

juniper – reasonably priced and without animal testing.
☎ 6238 8426 ⊠ B1-13 City-Link Mall ⏱ 10am-9.30pm Ⓜ City Hall

Stadium Royal Sporting House (4, D2)
Release your inner Federer at this tennis hub, or boost your world ranking in soccer, swimming, golf or aerobics with top-notch gear. Shoe brands (Puma, Nike, Adidas etc) line the walls, manufactured at bargain-basement prices in neighbouring China, Vietnam and Thailand.
☎ 6538 8888 ⊠ B2-15/23 Ngee Ann City, 391 Orchard Rd ⏱ 11am-9.30pm Thu-Sun, 11am-10pm Fri-Sat Ⓜ Orchard, Somerset

Yue Hwa Chinese Products (5, B1)
This five-storey department store stocks everything Chinese, from porcelain teapots and jade jewellery to slinky silk cheongsam, dried fish and medicinal herbs/fungi/spices. Pick up some ginseng, a snakeskin drum or a jar full of seahorses for the road.
☎ 6538 4222 ⊠ 70 Eu Tong Sen St ⏱ 11am-9pm Ⓜ Chinatown

and a pinch of bird's nest…Eu Yan Sang

Eating

Food, glorious food! Hurl a pair of chopsticks in any direction in Singapore and chances are they'll land in something edible. All kinds of international cuisine line the city's collective stomach, but Chinese, Indian, Malay and regional Peranakan dishes (a combination of Chinese and Malay ingredients and methods) are what you're here for. Each ethnic group has its own food rules; if you're unsure, look around and see what everybody else is doing (it's OK to ask for a fork!). See the boxed text on p51 for some must-try local suggestions.

For Singaporeans, what's on the plate is more important than the service or quality of the china. The slickest businessperson is just as comfortable sitting on a cheap plastic chair wading into a $3 plastic plate of *char kway teow* (broad noodles fried with sweet soy sauce) as they are eating $50 crabs in an air-conditioned restaurant. Even the swankiest spots offer economical set lunches.

Reservations are essential for upmarket eateries; a smart-casual dress code usually applies (no shorts, rude Hawaiian shirts or sandals). A service charge will be added to your bill; additional tipping is optional.

All restaurants (except hawker stalls) are nonsmoking. Whichever you choose – a meal for $2, $20 or $200 – you'll never walk away feeling hungry. Leave your diet at the door and grab a bowlful!

PRICE RANGES

Price ranges are based on what you're likely to spend per person for a one- to two-course meal with a nonalcoholic drink. A bottle of wine with your meal can double the bill!

$$$$	over $70
$$$	$36-70
$$	$10-35
$	under $10

Curry heaven at Tekka Centre, Little India (p51)

CHINATOWN

Blue Ginger (5, B3)
Peranakan $$
Blue Ginger serves traditional Peranakan cuisine in a woody shophouse. Trademark dishes include beef *rendang* (in coconut-milk curry sauce) and *udang ketak nana lemak* (crayfish with pineapple and coconut milk). Finish courageously with the house dessert – durian *chendol* (mung beans with green jelly, coconut milk and palm sugar). ☎ 6222 3928 ✉ 97 Tanjong Pagar Rd ⏰ noon-2.30pm & 6.30-10.30pm Ⓜ Tanjong Pagar Ⓚ fair Ⓥ some options

Broth (5, B3)
European Fusion $$$
In a leafy oasis atop sleepy Duxton Hill, this welcoming old shophouse has friendly staff, bentwood chairs, ceiling fans and a wall of wine and cookbooks. Candlelit dining outside is altogether romantic. Try the lamb loin followed by the chocolate torte with raspberries. ☎ 6323 3353 ✉ 21 Duxton Hill ⏰ noon-2.30pm & 6.30-10.30pm Mon-Fri, 6-10.30pm Sat Ⓜ Tanjong Pagar Ⓥ some options

Da Paolo E Judie (5, A3)
Italian $$$
Hats off to designer Mok Wei Wei for the sleek, romantically lit interior that makes this place look a million dollars – which is also what your bill will look like (just kidding). Seafood and pasta are the focus; try the lobster egg pasta or the famed cuttlefish risotto. There's a more homely branch, **Da**

Paolo** (5, C2; ☎ 6224 7081; 80 Club St).
☎ 6225 8306 ✉ 81 Neil Rd ⏰ 11am-2.30pm & 6.30-10.30pm Ⓜ Outram Park Ⓥ some options

Ember (5, A2)
Asian-European Fusion $$$
Downstairs at Hotel 1929, Ember glows with happy hipsters tucking into classy cuisine. Satisfying dishes like the slow-roasted rack of lamb with melted leek and potato fondant are sublime. The set lunch ($35) and dinner ($45) take you on a tour of the menu. ☎ 6347 1928 ✉ Hotel 1929, 50 Keong Saik Rd ⏰ 11.30am-2pm & 6.30-10pm Mon-Fri, 6.30-10pm Sat Ⓜ Outram Park

L'Aigle d'Or (5, B3)
French $$$$
Fit for Louis XIV, L'Aigle d'Or's gilt pilasters, wooden wall panels, intimate atmosphere and hefty dollar signs all spell 'special occasion'. A heavenly progression: foie gras (goose-liver pâté), quail *confit* (cooked, salted quail preserved in its own fat), French farm cheeses. Set lunches range from $28 to $58. ☎ 6327 8318 ✉ 83 Duxton Rd ⏰ noon-2pm & 7-10pm Ⓜ Tanjong Pagar

L'Angelus (5, C2)
French $$
Sophisticated French restaurants punctuate Chinatown's backstreets – comfort-food staples at this atmospheric, unpretentious bistro make it one of the better ones. Launch into the chicken liver salad, the mustard pork fillet and its

famous hot chocolate cake. ☎ 6225 6897 ✉ 85 Club St ⏰ noon-2.30pm & 6.30-10.30pm Ⓜ Chinatown

My Dining Room (5, C2)
Modern European Fusion $$$
Recently renovated (not that there was anything wrong with it before), My Dining Room sports a seasonal menu, shifting from classic French onion soup with ricotta dumplings to seafood lasagne, in a quasi-industrial but not unromantic setting. ☎ 6327 4990 ✉ 81B Club St ⏰ noon-3pm & 6.30-10.30pm Mon-Fri, 6.30-10.30pm Sat Ⓜ Chinatown

Qun Zhong Eating House (5, B2)
Chinese $
Lunchtime queues conga onto the street for seafood, pork and vegetable dumplings expertly rolled by the old ladies up the back of this shophouse. A plateful (steamed or fried) is $8, Chinese pizza is $10. ☎ 6221 3060 ✉ 21 Neil Rd ⏰ 11.30am-3pm & 5.30-9.30pm Thu-Tue Ⓜ Outram Park Ⓚ Ⓥ

Senso (5, C2)
Italian $$$
Sensuous Senso lays claim to being Singapore's top restaurant. After a pre-dinner drink in the lustrous bar, retreat to the courtyard for trad dishes like osso bucco (braised veal shank) and homemade mushroom veal ravioli. Wine list: long; service: immaculate; music: very *Godfather*. ☎ 6224 3534 ✉ 21 Club St ⏰ noon-3pm & 6-11pm Mon-Fr, 6-11pm Sat & Sun Ⓜ Chinatown Ⓚ fair Ⓥ some options

Soup Restaurant (5, B2)
Chinese $$

One of 11 'Soups' around town, this snug room features traditional round wooden tables and cute little chairs. House specialities are the double-boiled medicinal soups which (amongst other things) prevent coldness and cure 'windiness'. Try the snow frog with ginseng!
☎ 6222 9923 ✉ 25 Smith St ⏰ noon-2pm & 6-9.30pm Ⓜ Chinatown ♿ Ⓥ some options

Yum Cha Restaurant (5, B1)
Chinese Yum Cha $$

A cavernous place with broad clattering floorboards and grumpy trolley ladies serving from early till late – there's no excuse for going hungry! Munch into bite-sized prawn and abalone or 'crystal chive' dumplings at bite-sized prices. Sensational.
☎ 6372 1717 ✉ 02-01, 20 Trengganu St ⏰ 8am-11pm Ⓜ Chinatown ♿ good ♿

COLONIAL DISTRICT

Armenian Kopitiam (3, C5)
Café $

Scungy walls, red plastic chairs, exposed plumbing, cigarette butts, rattling ceiling fans, irritable cooks and clattering woks – this joint celebrates everything Singapore tries so hard to purge. Grab some *char kway teow* and a viscous Chinese coffee.
☎ 6339 6575 ✉ 34 Armenian St ⏰ 7am-9pm Ⓜ City Hall ♿ fair ♿

Baccarat (3, D4)
Asian Buffet $$

There are so many windows enveloping this fish-bowl restaurant they've had to erect bamboo screens to provide some intimacy. But looking out or looking in, the food looks fantastic! Tall-hatted chefs waltz around the central kitchen, keeping the buffet overflowing.
☎ 6884 9929 ✉ 51 Bras Basah Rd ⏰ 11am-2.30pm,
6.30-10pm Ⓜ Dhoby Ghaut ♿ good Ⓥ

Bobby Rubinos (3, D5)
American Grill $$

It's undeniably mainstream, but this is *the* place for ribs – put some meat on yours with reasonably priced burgers, steaks and other delights. Happy-hour beer, a pool table and breezy courtyard dining add weight to Bobby's cred.
☎ 6337 5477 ✉ B1-03 Fountain Court, CHIJMES, 30 Victoria St ⏰ noon-10.30pm Ⓜ City Hall ♿ Good ♿

Christa & Naomi (CAN) Café (3, E4)
Café $

Crowded with weird furniture and second-hand gas masks, telephones and abacuses, this CAN-do café is a remedy for Singaporean rigidity. Twenty-somethings smoke, drink beer and munch pizzas, noodles, cakes and curries. Music drifts from jazz to trance.
☎ 6337 3732 ✉ 01-12/13/14, 1 Liang Seah St ⏰ 4pm-2am Mon-Fri, 3pm-3am Sat & Sun Ⓜ Bugis ♿

Equinox (3, D5)
Asian & European $$$

Whoa! Adjectives struggle to cope with the jaw-dropping views from this 70th-floor restaurant. Soaring ceilings, Asiatic wall hangings and plush fabrics are mere backdrops. The view rates a 10, the food a little less. Book early for a window seat; dress sharp.
☎ 6837 3322 ✉ L70, Swissôtel The Stamford, 2 Stamford Rd ⏰ noon-2.30pm & 7-11pm Ⓜ City Hall ♿ good Ⓥ some options

---

BRUNCH & HIGH TEA
Modern Singapore has inherited the Brits' passion for toffy champagne brunches and highbrow high teas. Prices range from $50 to $90 per head, but kids often eat for free; ask about child-minding facilities. To be assured of a seat, book several days ahead. Try the oh-so-colonial **Billiard Room** at the Raffles Hotel (p52); champagne brunch at the **Hilton** (4, B2; ☎ 6730 3390; 581 Orchard Rd); waterfront **Post** (p63); **One-Ninety** at the Four Seasons hotel (p71); or the **Marmalade Pantry** (p57).

HAWKER FOOD

Essential to any Singapore visit is at least one hawker-centre meal, washed down with a cold bottle of Tiger beer. Hawker staples (generally $3 to $7) include laksa, *roti prata* (flaky, flat bread dipped into curry), Hainanese chicken rice, *char kway teow* (broad noodles fried with sweet soy sauce), *hokkien mee* (yellow wheat noodles fried with seafood, eggs and meat), *popiah* (spring rolls), *nasi lemak* (rice boiled in coconut milk, served with small fried fish, chicken and peanuts), *char siew* (roast pork) rice, *kaya* toast (toast with egg-and-coconut-cream jam) and *nasi padang* (rice with assorted Indonesian dishes). Here's a bowlful of the best centres, many of them operating 24/7; make like a local and join the longest queue:

Adam Road Food Centre (2, E4; cnr Adam & Dunearn Rds) Hawker food in-the-round, just beyond the Botanic Gardens. Try the *char kway teow* or barbecued stingray.

Chinatown Complex Food Centre (5, B2; cnr Sago & Trengganu Sts) One-hundred-and-fifty cheap, grungy and magically authentic stalls; chances are you'll be the only tourist in sight. Wash down some roast duck and rice with a condensed-milk *kopi* (coffee).

Geylang Serai Market (2, G4; Changi Rd) A truly authentic Singapore experience, with delicious Malay delicacies; the *nasi padang* is worth writing home about.

Lau Pa Sat (3, D8; cnr Raffles Quay & Cross St) Steamed dim sum and chilli crab, and sizzling satay for 40¢ a pop, all under a magnificent wrought-iron structure imported from Glasgow in 1894.

Lavender Food Centre (3, E1; Jl Besar) Much less touristed than most and staying open until the wee hours. The wonton noodles are worth queuing for.

Maxwell Road Food Centre (5, B2; Maxwell Rd) A breezy open-sided food hall with 103 stalls. Locals rack up empty Tiger bottles next to chubby school kids who obviously spend too much time here.

New Bugis Food Village (3, E4; Bugis St Market) Malay, Indonesian, Thai, Chinese and an embarrassing 'Western' food outlet. It's stifling during the day, the pink plastic chairs taking on surreal appeal.

Newton Food Centre (3, A1; Newton Circus) Gets a good rap from locals and tourists alike, though the touting can be a little over the top. Try the barbecued oysters.

Tekka Centre (3, D2, Serangoon Rd) A hectic, malodorous wet market with Indian, Muslim, Sri Lankan and vegetarian food stalls; don't miss the *roti prata*.

Garibaldi (3, E4)

Italian $$$

Swish, sequestered Garibaldi is about as Italian as Singapore gets: Italian chefs, 250 different Italian wines and Italian staff. The menu is *classico;* try the antipasti or homemade *tortellini di zucca* (pumpkin tortellini with sage butter, raisins and nutmeg). *Squisito!*
☎ 6837 1468 ✉ 36 Purvis St ⏰ noon-2.30pm & 6.30-10.30pm Ⓜ City Hall ♿ fair Ⓥ some options

Dress snappy to match the décor at Equinox (opposite)

Imperial Herbal Restaurant (3, E5)
Chinese $$

The in-house Chinese physician checks your pulse, examines your tongue then prescribes something on the menu to rebalance your yin and yang. Boost your libido, lose the zits, or stop the grey hair onslaught – something tasty will save the day!

☎ 6337 0491 ✉ L3 Metropole Hotel, 41 Seah St ⏲ 11.30am-2.30pm & 6.30-10.30pm Ⓜ City Hall ♿ good Ⓥ

Lei Garden (3, D5)
Hong Kong Cantonese $$$

Innumerable reception-ists frantically take phone reservations at this popular, elegant eatery. The wall-length fish tank glows behind round tables packed with business types and feasting Chinese families. Set menus range from $55 to $98; lunchtime dim sum (small serves of fried and steamed dumplings) is a winner.

☎ 6339 3822 ✉ 01-24 CHIJMES, 30 Victoria St ⏲ 11.30am-2.30pm & 6-10pm Ⓜ City Hall ♿ good ♿ Ⓥ

Raffles Hotel (3, D5)
Asian & European $-$$$$

Sidle up to a table at one of Raffles' ace eateries and pretend you're staying upstairs. There's the kid-friendly Seah Street Deli, dim sum at the Empire Café, Doc Cheng's curtained cubicles and 'trans-ethnic' cuisine or the plantation-meets-Perana-kan Long Bar Steakhouse. The Billiard Room doles out afternoon tea.

☎ 6337 1886 ✉ Raffles Hotel, 1 Beach Rd ⏲ noon-2pm & 7-10pm Ⓜ City Hall ♿

Rang Mahal (3, E5)
Indian $$$

Much-praised Indian in sophisticated stone and teak subcontinental surrounds. The vegetarian selection offers silky dhal dishes, while we can confirm the scarlet masala prawns are 'gutsy' rather than 'gusty' as the menu suggests. Graze through the tasting menu for $85.

☎ 6333 1788 ✉ L3 Pan Pacific Hotel, 7 Raffles Blvd ⏲ noon-2.30pm & 6.30-10.30pm Sun-Fri, 6-30-10.30pm Sat Ⓜ City Hall Ⓥ

Sakana (3, E4)
Japanese $$

Sakana is one of those great little informal eateries you so rarely find outside Japan – super-compact and uncomplicated with tiny screened booths, calligraphic art and rattling racks of sake bottles. Try the set lunch for $15.

☎ 6336 0266 ✉ 01-03/04 1 Liang Seah St ⏲ 11.30am-2.30pm & 6-10.30pm Ⓜ Bugis

Sanur (3, E5)
Indonesian $$

It's hard to ignore Sanur's beef *rendang,* a classically hewn Indonesian indulgence; the fragrant *ayam bali* (chicken in lemongrass curry) might take your mind off the Fountain of Wealth outside. There's another branch at Ngee Ann City.

☎ 6338 2777 ✉ B1-010 Suntec City ⏲ 11.45am-2.30pm & 6-9.30pm Ⓜ Bugis ♿ fair Ⓥ

Wing Seong Fatty's (Albert) Restaurant (3, D3)
Chinese $$

Standing the test of time, Fatty's has been knocking around various Albert St locations since 1926. Today's incarnation fills with flight crews tucking into the signature chicken clay pot (with special spicy sauce!). Backed by glazed ducks in the window, the outdoor terrace is perfect for people-watching.

☎ 6338 1087 ✉ 01-31 Burlington Sq, cnr Albert & Bencoolen Sts ⏲ noon-2.30pm & 5.15-10.15pm Ⓜ Bugis ♿ good ♿ Ⓥ some options

Doc Cheng's, one of the restaurants at Raffles Hotel

EAST COAST

328 Katong Laksa (2, G4)
Hawker Stall $
This uninspiring-looking nook redeems itself with what it claims to be the best laksa in Singapore. Not an uncommon assertion, but in this case it's possibly justified. Pull up a kerbside stool and measure the creamy concoction's virtues.
☎ 9732 8163 ⊠ 216 East Coast Rd ⏰ 8.30am-9pm Ⓜ Eunos, then taxi or walk 🚌 10, 12, 14, 40 ♿

Charlie's Peranakan Food (2, G4)
Peranakan $$
When chef Charlie Tan retired 10 years ago, people kept begging him to cook for them – so he went back into business! The essential Peranakan dish is *ayam buah keluak* (chicken with black nut) – Charlie's version is brilliant. The funky nut is baked in Indonesian volcanic ashes then shipped to Singapore.
☎ 6344 8824 ⊠ 205 East Coast Rd ⏰ 11.30am-2.30pm & 5.30-9.30pm Mon-Fri, noon-9.30pm Sat & Sun Ⓜ Eunos, then taxi or walk 🚌 10, 12, 14, 40 ♿ Ⓥ

East Coast Seafood Centre (2, G4)
Seafood $-$$$
Overlooking the Strait of Singapore, in the salty breeze,

Singaporean laksa

this renowned seafood centre boasts eight excellent Chinese and Thai restaurants, all with outdoor seating. Don't miss the chilli crabs and the intoxicating 'drunken' prawns.
⊠ 1202 East Coast Parkway ⏰ 5pm-midnight Ⓜ Bedok, then taxi 🚌 16, 36 ♿ good ♿

Guan Hoe Soon (2, G4)
Peranakan $$
This modest brick-fronted restaurant is the oldest Peranakan restaurant in Singapore. Lee Kuan Yew gets his takeaways here – Lee-baby recommends the *sotong assam goreng* (fried squid in sour sauce) on lettuce leaves or the Peranakan staple *ayam buah keluak*.
☎ 6344 2761 ⊠ 214 Joo Chiat Rd ⏰ 11am-2.30pm & 6-9.30pm Wed-Mon Ⓜ Eunos, then taxi or walk ♿ fair

Just Greens Vegetarian Food (2, G4)
Vegetarian $
You know the vegetarian food is good when you're bumping elbows with Buddhist monks. Peruse the dining-room

menu, or pick and choose from the $3 selections at the door (pumpkin, spinach, eggplant and noodle combos) and bring it inside.
☎ 6345 0069 ⊠ 49/51 Joo Chiat Pl ⏰ 8am-10pm Ⓜ Eunos, then taxi or walk ♿ Ⓥ

Mango Tree (2, G4)
Indian $$$
This tasteful restaurant in a strip of trashy fast foodies specialises in Keralan and Goan Indian cuisine. Splash on some mosquito repellent and hit the terrace for the Malabar seafood platter or the garlic crab. Squeeze in a cooling mango sorbet for dessert, then walk it off along the beach.
☎ 6442 8655 ⊠ 1000 East Coast Parkway ⏰ noon-2.30pm & 6.30-10.30pm Ⓜ Eunos, then taxi 🚌 16, 36

No Signboard Seafood (2, F4)
Seafood $$
The irony of the 30ft crustacean-emblazoned neon signboard seems to escape the diners – they're too busy munching into plates of white pepper crab under a fluoro-lit marquee. There's another branch at the East Coast Seafood Centre (left).
☎ 6842 3415 ⊠ 414 Geylang Rd ⏰ noon-2am Ⓜ Aljunied ♿ fair ♿

TAKING CARE OF BUSINESS
Looking to seal a deal over lunch with attentive service, upper-crust food and a tasteful, discreet setting? Try the following: Lei Garden (opposite), Jiang-Nan Chun (p56), Mezza9 (p57) or the Long Bar Steakhouse (p52) at Raffles. Don't forget to book ahead!

LITTLE INDIA & KAMPONG GLAM

Andhra Curry (3, D2)
Indian $$
This easygoing restaurant prides itself on fiery recipes from the Indian state Andhra Pradesh. Order up some Andhra Hyderabadi biryani (rice cooked with meat, seafood or vegetables), or absorb a flavoursome punch from the lamb dry curry. On Sunday night it's mayhem! ☎ 6293 3935 ✉ 41 Kerbau Rd ☺ 11.30am-3.30pm & 6-10.30pm Mon-Fri, 11.30am-10.30pm Sat & Sun Ⓜ Little India Ⓖ good Ⓖ Ⓥ

Banana Leaf Apolo (3, D2)
Indian $$
Fish-head curry sounds mildly disconcerting but, as the taxi drivers who eat here profess, there's a lot of delicious meat on those fishy cheeks! Can't face a fish face? Standards like *rogan josh* (tomato and red-pepper lamb curry) and lamb vindaloo (very spicy Central- or South-Indian curry) are less confronting. ☎ 6296 5995 ✉ 54/58 Race Course Rd ☺ 10.30am-10.30pm Ⓜ Little India Ⓖ Ⓥ

Popiah (spring rolls) are a traditional Nonya dish

Bumbu (3, E3)
Indonesian $$
In the shadows of the Sultan Mosque, endearing Bumbu's upstairs dining room pairs traditional furnishings with a giant antique gramophone. Try the *tahu telor* (egg and tofu with peanut sauce) and finish up with a gooey *chendol* (mung beans with green jelly, coconut milk and palm sugar). ☎ 6392 8628 ✉ 44 Kandahar St ☺ 11am-3pm & 6-10pm Ⓜ Bugis Ⓖ

Café Le Caire (3, E4)
Egyptian $
Once you start eating at this Egyptian café you need an iron will to stop. Try the spring chicken in yogurt and olive oil, the sweet and sticky *harissa,* or the *ba'mia* (lamb and okra stew); leave space for coffee and pastries. At night the old guys puff on *sheesha* (water pipes) and dissect the day. ☎ 6292 0979 ✉ 39 Arab St ☺ 11am-3am Ⓜ Bugis Ⓖ fair Ⓖ Ⓥ

Dosa Corner (3, D2)
Indian Vegetarian $
This lurid-lit place is wicked. Wash your hands at the basin near the counter then chow down on 2ft-long, rolled paper *dosa* (crispy pancakes) stuffed with funky potato, turmeric and onion masala. ☎ 6297 6297 ✉ 70 Serangoon Rd ☺ 8am-10.30am Ⓜ Little India Ⓖ fair Ⓖ Ⓥ

El Sheik (3, F3)
Lebanese $$
Desert hues wash over El Sheik, an up-market option on the fringe of Kampong Glam. If the English Premier League in the front dining room proves distracting, take your tub of blue Mediterranean honey (!) and jaw-clenchingly

Tucking into fish-head curry and vegetables

strong coffee and head for the palm-fringed, lantern-lit roof terrace.

☎ 6296 9116 ✉ cnr Pahang & Aliwal Sts ⏲ 11am-1am Ⓜ Bugis Ⓥ

French Stall (3, E1)
French $$

A cross-cultural gem! French chef Xavier Le Henaff married a Singaporean and set up this place for regular folks – the best of France (good wine, great food, better desserts and lilting accordion music) merged with Singaporean affordability and no-frills outdoor dining. In the afternoon there's desserts and drinks, dinner is served from 6pm. No reservations; cash only.

☎ 6299 3544 ✉ 544 Serangoon Rd ⏲ 3-6pm & 6-10pm Tue-Sun Ⓜ Farrer Park ♿ fair, bathrooms inaccessible ♿

Komala Vilas (3, D2)
Indian Vegetarian $

Wildly popular Komala Vilas serves terrific, cheap vegetarian meals all day long. Snack on spicy samosas (stuffed pastries) or *bonda* (deep-fried potato), or order the *thali* – a melange of veggie curries, dhal and condiments served on a banana leaf (scoop it up with your right hand).

☎ 6293 6980 ✉ 76/78 Serangoon Rd ⏲ 7am-10.30pm Ⓜ Little India ♿ Ⓥ

Samar Café (3, E3)
Middle Eastern $$

This corner café's menu rides a magic carpet across the Arabic world. Moroccan lanterns cast intricate shadows across black-and-white floor tiles and plush leather

EGALITARIAN VEGETARIAN

Most decent restaurants offer at least a few vegetarian options – call first to see what's cookin'. Otherwise, Little India (opposite) is packed with affordable veggie curry joints and you'll find vegetarian Chinese in Chinatown (p49) and the East Coast (p53). For superb modern Australian-style vegetarian food and sparkling service, taxi across town to Original Sin (p57) in Holland Village.

Mee rebus – thick noodles and spicy sweet potato gravy

couches as *sheesha* bubble in smoky corners. Food quality can be erratic – the mood compensates.

☎ 6398 0530 ✉ cnr Kandahar & Baghdad Sts ⏲ 24hr Ⓜ Bugis ♿ fair

Zam Zam (3, E3)
Indian $

These guys have been here since 1908, so we figure they probably know what they're doing. Tenure hasn't bred complacency – the touts attempt to herd moving cars through the door as frenetic chefs whip up mutton-, chicken- or vegetable-filled *murtabaks* (stuffed flaky, flat bread).

☎ 6298 7011 ✉ 699 North Bridge Rd ⏲ 7am-11pm Ⓜ Bugis ♿ Ⓥ

ORCHARD ROAD AREA

Au Jardin Les Amis (2, E4)
French $$$$
Oft voted Singapore's best restaurant, this is lofty French fare (frogs legs, *foie gras* and truffles) with transcontinental interlopers like tiramisu, ocean-trout *ceviche* (raw fish marinated in lime juice with olive oil and spices) and Iranian caviar, served with garden views. Dress to the nines; bookings essential.
☎ 6466 8812 ✉ EJH Corner House, Singapore Botanic Gardens, 1 Cluny Rd ⏰ 11.30am-2pm Sun, noon-2pm Fri, 7-9.30pm daily 🚌 7, 105, 123, 174, 502

Chatterbox (4, D2)
Hainanese $$
The aesthetic is uncompromisingly 'hotel lobby', but Chatterbox's chicken rice is the stuff of legend. Boiled chicken is plunged into ice to keep the flesh tender then served cold with warm broth, fragrant rice, rich dark soy, chilli and freshly ground ginger.
☎ 6831 6291 ✉ South Tower Lobby, Mandarin Singapore, 333 Orchard Rd ⏰ 5am-12.30am Ⓜ Somerset 🚻 Ⓥ some options

Orchard Rd scoffing

Gordon Grill (4, C1)
Steakhouse $$$
Suffering an endless '80s hangover with lashings of pinkish beige, the Goodwood Park Hotel needs a facelift. Forgiving carnivores queue for Australian Wagyu beef – lovingly hand-reared, milk fed and sold by 100g weight. Moo.
☎ 6730 1744 ✉ Goodwood Park Hotel, 22 Scotts Rd ⏰ noon-2.30am & 7-10.30pm Ⓜ Orchard

Graffiti Café (4, E2)
Café $
Teens doodle on the tabletops at this cosy café, jammed between the Heeren's microboutiques. Bowls of handmade

wanton noodles and cheap curries clatter across heartfelt 'I love Elaine's ass' and 'Free Sex!' dedications.
☎ 6238 0422 ✉ 05-29 The Heeren, 260 Orchard Rd ⏰ 11am-9pm Ⓜ Somerset 🚻 fair 🚻

Halia (2, E4)
Asian & European $$$
Bedecked with natural timbers, this airy, laid-back oasis nestles into a nook of the Botanic Gardens. House faves include soft-shell black-pepper crab and the special curry chicken. Plunder the fully stocked bar and head for the terrace.
☎ 6476 6711 ✉ Ginger Garden, Singapore Botanic Gardens, 1 Cluny Rd ⏰ 8am-11.15pm, noon-3pm, tea 3-5pm, 6.30-11pm 🚌 7, 105, 123, 174, 502 🚻 good 🚻 Ⓥ

Jiang-Nan Chun (4, B2)
Cantonese $$$
The conscious colour departure from traditional red/gold interiors to brooding black signals a revolutionary state of mind. Four specialised

Pepper crab is a favourite with locals

menus (including vegetarian and 'healthy Chinese') are bolstered by a fabulous wine list and impeccable service. The marinated crab claws are show-stoppers.
☎ 6734 1110 ✉ Four Seasons, 190 Orchard Blvd ⏲ 11.30am-2.30pm & 6-10.30pm Ⓜ Orchard ♿ good Ⓥ

Killiney Kopitiam (4, F3)
Café $
The waiter yells your order at ear-splitting volume and the coffee – shaken by the resulting seismic disturbance – inevitably arrives erupted into the saucer. This Singaporean institution is *the* place for a '*KOPI!!*' and '*KAYA TOOOAST!!!*' breakfast.
☎ 6734 9648 ✉ 67 Killiney Rd ⏲ 6am-11pm Mon & Wed-Sat, 6am-6pm Tue & Sun Ⓜ Somerset ♿

Marmalade Pantry (4, B2)
Café $$
Crisp white tablecloths, comfy booths and glossy mags set the scene at this sub-street café serving tasty (if pricey) morsels. This is about as soothing and tasteful as a mall eatery is gonna get. Yuppies flock for Sunday brunch.
☎ 6734 2700 ✉ B1-08 Palais Renaissance, 390 Orchard Rd ⏲ 11.30am-9.30pm Mon-Fri, 10am-9.30pm Sat, 10am-4pm Sun Ⓜ Orchard ♿ good ♿ Ⓥ

Mezza9 (4, C2)
International $$$
Lobsters on ice, baskets of Tabasco Sauce bottles, glazed wine–cool rooms, floor-to-ceiling windows and six open kitchens so you can watch the flames under your wok – there's plenty to look at,

and plenty of suits doing the looking.
☎ 6738 1234 ✉ Grand Hyatt, 10/12 Scotts Rd ⏲ 11am-11pm Ⓜ Orchard ♿ Good Ⓥ

Original Sin (2, E4)
Modern Mediterranean $$$
Holland Village is a fair hike from Orchard Rd, but this place is worth it. The sinful menu roams from crispy porcini polenta to veggie burgers and excellent risottos with an expansive/expensive Antipodean wine list. Book a mosaic-topped terrace table.
☎ 6475 5605 ✉ 01-62 Jln Merah Saga, Block 43 Chip Bee Gardens, Holland Village ⏲ 11.30am-2.30pm & 6-10.30pm 🚌 7, 61, 77 ♿ outside only Ⓥ some options

Samy's Curry Restaurant (2, E4)
Indian $
For 25 years the ceiling fans have spun above Samy's munificent curries in this leafy, open-walled, timber-shuttered colonial throwback. The fish-head curry is sublime, or wolf down chicken, lamb and vego delights. Come early for a veranda table.
☎ 6472 2080 ✉ Civil Service Club, Block 25 Dempsey Rd ⏲ 11am-11pm 🚌 7, 77, 105, 106, 123, 174 ♿ Ⓥ

YOU WANT VIEWS WITH THAT?
For an awesome bird's-eye perspective, you can't beat Equinox (p50) or Si Chuan Dou Hua (p59). Waterfront breezes waft through Quays' restaurants such as Indo-Chine Waterfront (p58), Pierside Kitchen & Bar (p59) and House of Sundanese Food (p58). For a greener scene try Halia (opposite) or Au Jardin Les Amis (opposite) at the Singapore Botanic Gardens.

Kopi, kaya toast and boiled eggs

THE QUAYS

Bon Gout (3, B6)
Japanese Café $$
This cheerily eccentric place (not to be misread as 'Bong-Out') is weird enough to be straight out of Tokyo. It's a second-hand bookshop-CD store hybrid full of students and literati, reading, laughing and slurping *ramen* soups, Japanese curries and Tiger beer (sometimes all at once). ☎ 6732 5234 ✉ 01-01 The Quayside, 60 Robertson Quay ⏰ noon-10pm 🚌 51, 64, 123, 186 ♿ good 🚻

Coriander Leaf (3, C6)
Asian Fusion $$$
Slide into a wicker chair far from Clarke Quay's madding architecture, and peruse a menu traversing Australian, Indian, Vietnamese, Thai and Japanese culinary stylings. Chef Sami (a Pakistani New Yorker) also runs cooking courses – see p39. ☎ 6732 3354 ✉ 02-03 Clarke Quay ⏰ noon-2pm & 6-10pm Mon-Fri, 6-10pm Sat Ⓜ Clarke Quay Ⓥ some options

House of Sundanese Food (3, C6)
Indonesian $$
A beacon of low-key amicability on hypertensioned Boat Quay; dine under the riverside boughs or upstairs surrounded by artefacts. Tickle your tonsils with the *ayam bumbu* (mildly spiced chicken in semi-sweet lemon gravy) or west-Javanese grilled sea bass, washed down with quenching lime juice. ☎ 6534 3775 ✉ 55/55A Boat Quay ⏰ 11am-2.30pm & 6-10pm Mon-Fri, 6-10pm Sat & Sun Ⓜ Raffles Place ♿ outdoors only Ⓥ

IndoChine Waterfront (3, D6)
Southeast Asian $$$
The IndoChine cartel's riverside operation boasts Boat Quay views and sumptuous surrounds – dark leather chairs and glittering chandeliers. The menu is a sophisticated brace of Viet-namese-, Cambodian- and Laotian-inspired dishes. You'll have a similar experience (at café prices) at **Siem Reap II** (☎ 6338 7596) next door. ☎ 6339 1720 ✉ Asian Civilisations Museum, 1 Empress Pl ⏰ noon-3pm & 6.30pm-12.30am Mon-Fri, 6.30pm-12.30am Sat & Sun Ⓜ Raffles Place ♿ good

Kinara (3, C6)
Punjabi $$
Kinara means 'river shore' in Punjabi. Take a riverside table or eat inside the renovated shophouse, decked-out like a *haveli* (ornately decorated Indian residence) with copper, iron, teak and sandstone. Try the tandoori *hari machli aftab* (boneless fish tikka marinated and cooked in the oven). ☎ 6533 0412 ✉ 57 Boat Quay ⏰ 11.30am-2.30pm & 6.30-10.30pm Ⓜ Raffles Place ♿ outdoors only 🚻 Ⓥ

My Humble House (3, E6)
Modern Chinese $$$
One of Singapore's most hyped restaurants, with

Not-so-bad views at IndoChine Waterfront

THE FOOD DETECTIVE
Cunningly disguised in a trench coat and dark glasses, flamboyant TV food detective **Makansutra** tracks down elusive hawker stalls and food centres in search of Singapore's best and brightest. You can pick up a copy of Makansutra's definitive hawker-food guide at good bookshops or check out www.makansutra.com for the latest reviews.

whimsical, absurdly oversized Chinese-style tables and chairs (the name is tongue-in-cheek). Business groups chow down on abalone, truffles and seafood on an elaborate but subtly flavoured Sichuan menu. Dress snazzy; reservations essential.

☎ 6423 1881 ✉ 02-27 The Esplanade, 8 Raffles Ave ⏰ noon-3pm & 6.30-11pm Ⓜ City Hall ♿ fair

Pierside Kitchen & Bar (3, D7)
Fusion Seafood $$$
Pierside's minimalist alfresco stylings earn the Singapore stamp of cool. Mirrored walls double the area the waiters need to cover – they glide around distributing plates of snapper pie, cumin-spiced crab cakes and lobster gumbo to well-heeled diners.

☎ 6438 0400 ✉ 01-01 One Fullerton, 1 Fullerton Rd ⏰ noon-3pm & 6-10pm Ⓜ Raffles Place ♿ good

Real Food Daily (3, B5)
Wholefood Café $$
The food here is indeed real – browse the chalkboard for delicious breakfasts, organic chicken tandoori burgers and wild king salmon steaks with green tea noodles, wasabi and sesame sauce. There's jazz, newspapers, good coffee and a deli out the back.

☎ 6733 8231 ✉ 5 Mohamed Sultan Rd ⏰ 10am-7pm Mon-Thu, 10am-9pm Fri & Sat, 9am-3pm Sun 🚌 33, 54, 139, 195 Ⓥ

Si Chuan Dou Hua (3, D7)
Chinese $$$-$$$$
Select one of 10 set menus ($40 to $180), then relax and absorb the bodacious 60th-floor views. Standout dishes like braised abalone with mushrooms and steamed king fish in soy sauce will temporarily tear your eyes away from the windows.

☎ 6535 6006 ✉ 60-01 UOB Plaza 1, 80 Raffles Pl

Little parcels of joy (aka dumplings) at the Hawker Centre

⏰ 11.30am-10.30pm Ⓜ Raffles Place ♿ good

Superbowl – The Art of Eating Congee (3, C6)
Chinese Congee $$
There aren't many American gridiron players here, but we did find dozens of MSG-free varieties of congee (semiliquid Chinese porridge). Try it with 'drunken' chicken, pigs' kidneys, preserved eggs, or a more appetising-sounding combo of your own.

☎ 6538 6066 ✉ 80 Boat Quay ⏰ noon-2.30pm & 6-10.30pm Mon-Sat Ⓜ Raffles Place ♿

Viet Lang (3, D6)
Vietnamese $$
Viet Lang's cool, captivating interior is filled with muttering parliamentarians and chatty locals enjoying the pho ga (white rice noodle soup), steamed snails stuffed with pork, soft-shell pepper crab and French-influenced desserts. It's perfect for a special occasion.

☎ 6337 3379 ✉ 01-03 Old Parliament House Annex, 1 Old Parliament Lane ⏰ 11.30am-11pm Ⓜ Raffles Place, Clarke Quay, City Hall Ⓥ

Satay sticks cooked the traditional wood-fired way

Entertainment

Singapore's nightlife gets a bum rap (mainly from Singapore Sling-swilling package tourists) but there's really no excuse for an early night in Singapore.

Most nocturnal bar activity bubbles up around the Quays, Circular Rd, Mohamed Sultan Rd and Chinatown, while CHIJMES is good for alfresco bars/eateries. Clubs generally close at 3am and are strictly drug-free; get your kicks instead from local acts and touring DJs who regularly stop off in Singapore. Dress is smart casual – no shorts or sandals.

The opera talent at the Chinese Theatre Circle (p68)

In contrast, the live music scene is woeful; cover bands, tinkling Richard Clayderman piano classics and karaoke bars rule the roost (how many times can you hear someone massacre Bryan Adams' *Heaven* in one week?).

Singaporeans adore the cinema – mainstream US blockbusters are standard fodder. The city's theatre scene is vibrant, staging everything from experimental originals to repertory standards. You'll also find plenty of classical and tourist-friendly opera performances.

Tickets for most events are available through **Sistic** (☎ 6348 5555; www.sistic.com.sg) or **TicketCharge** (☎ 6296 2929; www.ticketcharge.com.sg). For up-to-date listings see the *Straits Times* newspaper and *8 Days* magazine. For nightlife, pick up the free street mags *I-S* and *Juice* at cafés, hotels and music stores.

Chinese New Year's annual parade

SPECIAL EVENTS

Check out www.visitsingapore.com.sg for precise dates of special events.

January–February

Ponggal South Indian harvest thanksgiving parades, revolving around Little India and the Sri Mariamman Temple (p17).

Chinese New Year Dragon dances, fireworks and over-the-top parades in Chinatown.

Chingay Processions of lion dancers, floats and Chinese flag bearers parade along Orchard Rd.

Thaipusam Seriously devoted Hindus march from the Sri Srinivasa Perumal carrying *kavadi* (decorated metal frames hung from metal hooks and spikes driven into their flesh – no blood!).

March–April

Singapore International Film Festival Just what it says it is.

April–May

Vesak Day A celebration of all things Buddha: birth, death and enlightenment.

May–June

Dragon Boat Festival Boat-races cast a bubbling wake across Marina Bay.

Singapore Festival of Arts Held every even-numbered year.

Festival of Asian Performing Arts Held every odd-numbered year.

July–August

Singapore Food Festival A month-long culinary cacophony.

Great Singapore Sale A two-month shopping extravaganza zooming-in on Orchard Rd.

Singapore National Day Military pomp and civilian processions, plus fireworks, on 9 August.

Festival of the Hungry Ghosts The souls of the dead get their kicks on Earth (p26).

September–October

Thimithi A fire-walking ceremony; Hindu devotees hot-foot it over glowing coals at the Sri Mariamman Temple (p17).

October–November

Deepavali Little India is a month-long blaze of lights during this most important Hindu festival.

Festival of the Nine Emperor Gods Nine days of Chinese operas, processions and related events.

Hari Raya Puasa A three-day celebration marking the end of Ramadan, the month-long Muslim fast.

Singapore River Buskers Festival Bring your earplugs; see p67.

December

Hari Raya Haji Muslim festival honouring the conclusion of the pilgrimage to Mecca.

BARS & PUBS

Unless stated otherwise, entry to bars and pubs is free.

Alley Bar (4, E2)
Sky-high ceilings, dark timbers, candlelight and slick stylings paint this alleyway bar with restrained melodrama. Yuppies and expats converse in shadowy, cushioned nooks, quaffing wine and on-tap Belgian beers. Roam upstairs to **Rouge** (☎ 6732 6966) for a dance.
☎ 6738 8818 ✉ 2 Emerald Hill Rd ⏰ 5pm-2am Sun-Thu, 5pm-3am Fri & Sat Ⓜ Somerset

Bar Opiume (3, D6)
Opiume's gleaming glass bar fuses industrial chic with polished floorboards, oversized chandeliers and big-ass couches (not that the skinny clientele command any respect in that department). Seductive river views extend from painted wicker chairs on the terrace.
☎ 6339 2876 ✉ Asian Civilisations Museum, 1 Empress Pl ⏰ 5pm-2am Ⓜ Raffles Place ♿ fair

Bar Sá Vá nh (5, C2)
Sá Vá nh's soft candlelight sheds light on dusky shadows as gorgeous svelte things flit

by the fishpond; expats sink into sunken lounges; platters of Asian tapas make the rounds; and ambient tunes snake into the night – all under the heavy-lidded gaze of Buddha himself. ☎ 6323 0145 ✉ 49 Club St 🕒 3pm-2am Mon-Thu, 3pm-2am Fri & Sat 🇲 Chinatown

Dubliners – the pub of choice for James Joyce

BQ Bar (3, C6)
This quayside glass box fills with phone-wielding businessmen having one-way conversations about selling photocopiers. It's a bit uptight, but an awesome concrete bar and lilting jazz give it the edge over its Boat Quay brethren. Marathon happy hours run from 11.30am to 8pm.
☎ 6536 9722 ✉ 39 Boat Quay 🕒 11am-1am Mon & Tue, 11am-3am Wed-Sat, 5pm-midnight Sun 🇲 Clarke Quay, Raffles Place 🚻 fair

Dubliners (4, F2)
Lousy Irish pubs filled with bellowing, beer-bellied execs are omnipresent in Singapore, but this elegant white colonial place is a cut above

the fray. No sign of James Joyce, but toast his efforts with a pint of black stuff on the veranda.
☎ 6735 2220 ✉ Winsland Conservation House, 165 Penang Rd 🕒 11.30am-1am Sun-Thu, 11.30am-2am Fri & Sat 🇲 Somerset

En Bar & Lounge (3, B5)
The rather silly Japanese restaurant En has expanded into a bar, joining the Mohamed Sultan Rd booze brigade. The glam ambience of the outdoor area, mirrored music room and a retro lounge lure a lethargically 'money' crowd, all cigarettes and winks.
☎ 6732 6863 ✉ 01-59 UE Sq, Mohamed Sultan Rd 🕒 6pm-3am 🇲 Clarke

Quay 🚌 33, 54, 139, 195 🚻 fair

New Asia Bar (3, D5)
Singapore's most spectacular views join forces with a giant, curvilinear mother-of-pearl wall, soaring ceilings and VIP mezzanine for a drinking experience management insists will leave you 'charged'. The dance floor tilts a tricky 20 degrees – you might regret that last martini.
☎ 6831 5681 ✉ L71-72, Swissôtel The Stamford, 2 Stamford Rd 💲 Fri & Sat $25 🕒 3pm-late 🇲 City Hall 🚻 fair

Next Page (3, B5)
This is where Hunter S Thompson would have hung

Lou Reed and Mao hang out at Velvet Underground (opposite)

out if he'd been a journo in Singapore instead of San Juan. Dark timber bar, red lanterns, exposed brickwork, booths, pool table, Carlsberg on tap and quirky bartenders – sit down and write the next page of your novel.

☎ 6235 6967 ✉ 17 Mohamed Sultan Rd ☽ 3pm-3am Ⓜ Clarke Quay 🚌 33, 54, 139, 195

No 5 (4, E2)

Not much imagination went into naming this long-running boozer in a 1910 Peranakan shophouse. Expect retro-Asiatic touches, vats of chilli vodka and smoky snooker vibes. It's damn touristy around here, but the cool evening ambience is sweet relief from Orchard Rd. Neighbouring **Que Pasa** (☎ 6235 6626) and **Ice Cold Beer** (☎ 6735 9929) are the same but different.

☎ 6732 0818 ✉ 5 Emerald Hill Rd ☽ noon-2am Mon-Sat, 5pm-2am Sun Ⓜ Somerset

Post (3, D6)

After-workers schmooze beneath high ceilings, metallic Art Deco finishes and a wall of vodka – if only all post offices looked this snazzy! Things look even better after a few caipiroskas (vodka, lime juice and sugar syrup on ice) and a chubby Davidoff 'Short Perfector' from the humidor. Sunday brunch will cure your hangover (bookings essential).

☎ 6733 8388 ✉ Fullerton Hotel, 1 Fullerton Sq ☽ 3pm-2am Mon-Fri, 5pm-2am Sat & Sun, brunch noon-2pm Sun Ⓜ Raffles Place ♿ good

Sound Bar (3, A6)

Choose between alfresco riverside cocktails and beery bar stools by the glowing fish tank. Soporific tunes, evening breezes and sexy clientele round out the mood. Tramp upstairs to the Liquid Room (p65) later on. If you're feeling lucky, book a hotel room for the night.

☎ 6333 8117 ✉ Gallery Hotel, 76 Robertson Quay ☽ 6pm-3am Tue-Sat Ⓜ Clarke Quay 🚌 33, 54, 139, 195 ♿ good

Union Bar (5, C2)

With big squishy corduroy couches, plenty of elbow room and views onto Club St's passing parade, this joint is hard to beat for a relaxed late afternoon beer. Upstairs

is My Dining Room (p49) – perfect for dinner.

☎ 6327 4990 ✉ 81 Club St ☽ 3pm-1am Mon-Thu, 3pm-2am Fri, 5pm-2am Sat Ⓜ Chinatown

Velvet Underground (3, A5)

This Moroccan-inspired bar has multicoloured club lounges, Philippe Starck furniture and Keith Haring and Andy Warhol originals. You probably won't bump into Lou Reed, but it's still a classy joint – dress to kill and pack some cash. New York vibe, garage and commercial dance; admission for over-28s only.

☎ 6738 2988 ✉ Zouk, 17 Jiak Kim St 💲 incl 2 drinks & entry to Zouk & Phuture $35 ☽ 9pm-3.30am Tue-Sat

Exterior of Que Pasa Pub

CINEMAS

Singapore adores the movies. Non-English films are usually subtitled; admission prices vary according to session times. Weekend screenings sell out (even midnight sessions) so book ahead and be prepared to queue. Check the *Straits Times* for session details.

Alliance Française (3, A1)
A departure from standard Hollywood fare (and from Orchard Rd), Alliance unleashes classic and contemporary French films every Tuesday night. Prime with a wine in the on-site café. *C'est bon!*
☎ 6737 8422 ☐ www .alliancefrancaise.org.sg ✉ 1 Sarkies Rd 💲 from $8 🕒 8pm Tue Ⓜ Newton

GV Gold Class (2, E4)
Singapore's swankiest film house soothes you with plush carpeting, single and double reclining seats complete with footrests, table service and a reasonable menu. Recommended for romance and self-indulgence. Ahhhh…
☎ 1900 912 1234
☐ www.gv.com.sg ✉ 03-39/40 Great World City, 1 Kim Seng Pde 💲 tickets Mon-Fri $25, Sat & Sun $30 🕒 10am-midnight 🚌 16, 75, 195, 970 ♿ good 🚻

Lido (4, C2)
Follow the movie posters up to Lido's bewildering array of A- and B-grade Hollywood blockbusters. Similar stuff gets an airing at **Cathay Cineleisure** (4, D2; ☎ 6838 1030; www.tickets.cathay .com.sg; L5, 8 Grange Rd) down the road, and at **Golden Village** (3, C4; ☎ 6334 3766; www.gv.com .sg) at Plaza Singapura.
☎ 6732 4124, credit-card bookings 6738 0555 ☐ www.shaw.com.sg ✉ 05 Shaw House, 350 Orchard Rd 💲 from $8 🕒 10am-midnight Ⓜ Orchard ♿ Good 🚻

Omni Theatre (2, C3)
Omni projects 3D films (about space, mountains, dolphins etc) and Disney classics onto a 23m hemispheric screen and blasts your eardrums with 20,000 watts of sound. Intense! Snow City (p33) is next door if you need to cool down afterwards.
☎ 6425 2500 ☐ www .science.edu.sg ✉ 15 Science Centre Rd 💲 $10/5 🕒 11am, last show 8pm Ⓜ Jurong East 🚌 66, 178, 198, 335 ♿ good 🚻

Shaw Complex (3, E4)
Seating 1200 suitably impressed viewers in front of an enormous screen, this is the big daddy of Singapore cinemas. Major blockbusters and Chinese and local releases shimmer across the big screen. They also have a cinema at Bugis Junction.
☎ 6738 0555 ☐ www .shaw.com.sg ✉ Shaw Towers, 100 Beach Rd 💲 from $9 🕒 10am-midnight Ⓜ Bugis

CLUBS

Singapore's clubs are forever folding and revamping; check *I-S* magazine and *Juice* for reviews. Cover charges are hefty, but they usually include a drink or two. Happy hours and 'girls drink free' promotions are ubiquitous; gals usually pay lower covers than guys.

Babyface (3, D7)
Three levels of harbourside decadence: chill-out bar, band room and pumping disco. The house band's desperately unsexy stage posturing is unforgivable; clubbers don't seem to mind and order gin by the bottle. Baby-faced punters might not get in (admission for over-23s only).
☎ 6236 5120 ✉ 02-02 One Fullerton, 1 Fullerton Rd 💲 men/women $20/18 🕒 9pm-6am Tue-Sat, 9pm-11pm Mon & Sun Ⓜ Raffles Place ♿ fair

SINGAPORE INTERNATIONAL FILM FESTIVAL
Film fiends should check out the **Singapore International Film Festival** (SIFF; www.filmfest.org.sg), held at various cinemas around April. Expect a good range of international releases plus home-grown films unlikely to be seen elsewhere. Don't let the fact that *Zoolander* was banned in Singapore put you off.

Brix (4, C1)
If you make it past the goons on the door, you can spend the night lurching between the whisky bar (single-malt heaven), wine bar (namesake brickwork and impressive wine list) and music room (bands, R&B/disco/soul DJs and dancing).
☎ 6416 7292 ▫ www .singapore.grand.hyatt.com ✉ B1, Grand Hyatt Hotel, 10 Scotts Rd 💲 men/women $35/25 Thu-Sat 🕑 7pm-3am Ⓜ Orchard

Liquid Room (3, A6)
Less liquid, more gunmetal, this intimate club's industrial vibe and top DJs set the scene for serious dancing. If you make it past the queue, there's progressive house, tech-house and trance. Toilets are rare as pills – you might find yourself squirming on the spot regardless of the music.
☎ 6333 8117 ▫ www .liquidroom.com.sg ✉ Gallery Hotel, 76 Robertson Quay 💲 incl 2 drinks $20 🕑 11pm-3am Wed, Fri & Sat 🚌 33, 54, 139, 195

Ministry Of Sound (3, C6)
Those decadent Brits have finally made it to Singapore. The world's largest MOS proffers better than average whistles and bells: seven separate rooms, superb digital sound and light, a Travolta-esque chequered dance-floor, and a 20ft water curtain. Be prepared to queue. If you can't face the queue, head around the corner to **Attica** (☎ 6333 9973; www.attica.com.sg; 01-10/12/13/14 Clarke Quay; incl 2 drinks & entry to Attica Too $25; 🕑 5pm-3am

Fairy-lights outside Zouk on Jiak Kim St

Sun-Tue & Thu, till 4am Wed, Fri & Sat).
☎ 6333 9368 ▫ www .ministryofsound.com.sg ✉ 01-07 Block C Clarke Quay 💲 men/women $15-25/free-20 🕑 9pm-3am Wed-Sat Ⓜ Clarke Quay

RAV (3, C6)
Unrelentingly red with disco balls aplenty, RAV is Circular Rd's stand-out club, pumping out everything from acid jazz to Motown for the under-30s. Big-name local DJ Illusion is a regular; gals are regular recipients of free-flow 'housepours'.
☎ 6327 4900 ▫ www .rav.com.sg ✉ 69 Circular Rd 💲 variable 🕑 6pm-3am Sun-Fri, 6pm-4am Sat Ⓜ Clarke Quay, Raffles Place

Zouk (3, A5)
Ibiza-inspired Zouk is a world-class contender and a regular destination for globe-trotting DJs. Five bars, 2000-capacity, roomy dance floor…there's guaranteed bar access and plenty of space to cut the rug. There's also the alfresco Zouk Wine Bar, old-school drum & bass at Phuture, the chic Velvet Underground (p63) and prodigious queues.
☎ 6738 2988 ▫ www .zoukclub.com.sg ✉ 17 Jiak Kim St 💲 $20-35 🕑 Zouk & Phuture 8pm-3.30am Wed, Fri & Sat; Wine Bar 6pm-3.30am Mon-Sun

THE DRUGS DON'T WORK
If you want to avoid returning home in a body bag, don't even think about taking drugs in Singapore or hanging out with anyone who does. Like neighbouring states, Singapore imposes the death penalty for trafficking, importing and exporting even relatively small amounts of illegal drugs. Don't risk it; get drunk instead.

THEATRE, CABARET & COMEDY

1 Nite Stand Comedy Club (3, C6)

'I just flew in from LA, and boy are my arms tired!' The comedy at this big, carpeted bar is marginally more sophisticated, with mostly overseas stand-ups hamming it up during the last week of every month.

☎ 6334 1954 🖳 www
.the1nitestand.com ✉ 01-15/20 Clarke Quay 💲 shows around $50 🕒 noon-2am
Ⓜ Clarke Quay ♿ fair

Action Theatre (3, D4)

The nonprofit Action theatre produces original works with contemporary themes. Its play *Mail Order Brides & Other Oriental Takeaways* was the first Singaporean play to be produced in New York. Nice one!

☎ 6837 0842 🖳 www.ac
tion.org.sg ✉ 42 Waterloo St 💲 varies Ⓜ City Hall

Gold Dust (4, B2)

Never seen a drag queen in traditional Thai dress lip-sync to Gloria Gaynor's *I Will Survive*? Lose your cherry with

I-S magazine, an entertainment guide to what's on (p88)

veteran drag queen Kumar, dancing and lip-syncing to everything from Canto-pop to Hindustani. Keep a low profile – things can get personal.

☎ 6235 7170 🖳 www
.thegolddustclub.com
✉ 02-11 Orchard Towers (rear block), 1 Claymore Dr
💲 $15-30 🕒 10pm Mon-Sat Ⓜ Orchard

Guinness Theatre (3, C5)

Part of the Substation experimental arts complex, this small theatre (painted exclusively in beery black) promotes local works by emerging Singaporean artists. To keep things accessible, most tickets are free or

require only a donation.

☎ 6337 7535 🖳 www
.substation.org ✉ 45 Armenian St 💲 by donation
🕒 box office noon-8.30pm Mon-Fri & 2 hr before shows Ⓜ City Hall

Necessary Stage (2, G4)

One of Singapore's best-known experimental theatre groups has a penchant for dark, earnest works, but it also does some great interactive and collaborative stuff with schools.

☎ 6440 8115 🖳 www
.necessary.org ✉ B1-02 Marine Parade Community Bldg, 278 Marine Parade Rd
💲 $20-35 🚌 12, 14, 32

Singapore Repertory Theatre (3, B5)

This company is the bigwig of Singapore's theatre scene; expect to see repertory standards such as *The Glass Menagerie, Hamlet* and *Death of a Salesman*, plus modern Singaporean works.

☎ 6733 8166 🖳 www
.srt.com.sg ✉ DBS Drama Centre, 20 Merbau Rd
💲 $30-80 Ⓜ Clarke Quay
🚌 33, 54, 139, 195

DRAMA QUEENS

Singapore's more dynamic and contemporary theatre groups produce edgy but accessible home-grown and international work at various venues around town. If you have time and opportunity, look for shows by **Theatreworks** (www.theatreworks.org.sg), **Toy Factory Ensemble** (www.toyfactory.org.sg) and Singapore's sexiest theatre company, **Wild Rice** (www.wildrice.com.sg). For classical Indian dance and vocal and instrumental music, check out the **Nrityalaya Aesthetics Society** (www.nas.org.sg).

LIVE MUSIC

Unlike the club scene, live music is not a happening thang in Singapore. It's hard to find local bands, and when you do they're usually churning out covers from the Michael Bolton–Peter Cetera collaborative song-book. Jazz is generally a safer bet than rock.

DON'T GIVE UP YOUR DAY JOB

Until recently, busking was illegal in Singapore, viewed as a sneaky form of begging rather than artistic expression. Today, wailing guitarists and puppeteers are commonplace in MRT tunnels and along Orchard Rd. Protagonists/antagonists can sign up for the annual Singapore River Buskers Festival in November; the only catch is they have to audition for a three-month licence and donate their earnings (after expenses) to charity.

Blue Note (3, C6)

Yep, the management sure thought long and hard about naming their jazz bar. Obvious, yes, but Blue Note does rain some classy musical atmospheria on Circular Rd's bleary, karaoke-strained parade. Good for an afternoon brew too.
☎ 6438 2282 🖵 www.bluenote.com.sg ✉ 48 Circular Rd 💲 free 🕓 noon-late Ⓜ Raffles Place ♿ fair

Crazy Elephant (3, C6)

Anywhere that bills itself as 'crazy' should raise alarm bells ringing, but you won't hear them once you're inside. Singapore's best blues bar is beery, blokey, low, loud, graffiti-covered and testosterone-heavy – rock on!
☎ 6337 1990 🖵 www.crazyelephant.com ✉ 01-07 Clarke Quay 💲 usually free 🕓 5pm-1am Sun-Thu, 3pm-2am Fri & Sat Ⓜ Clarke Quay ♿ good

Harry's Bar (3, D7)

Harry's jazzy blues mingles well with night-time river views, but somehow seems to miss the whole 'my woman left me and my dog ate my money' point of it all. It's a long way from the bayou, but not a bad spot for an ale.
☎ 6538 3029 ✉ 28 Boat Quay 🖵 www.harrys-bar.com.sg 💲 varies 🕓 11am-late, music from 10pm 💲 free Ⓜ Raffles Place ♿ fair

Jazz@Southbridge (3, C6)

Above Boat Quay, this intimate jazz bar sets plush sofas in front of a small stage. With the exception of a rather indulgent pianist, the house band is excellent, and well-known internationals often grace the stage. Sets kick off around 9.30pm.
☎ 6327 4671 🖵 www.southbridgejazz.com.sg ✉ 82B Boat Quay 💲 admission free, touring acts $15-20 🕓 5.30pm-1am Tue-Thu, 5.30pm-2am Fri & Sat, 6pm-1am Sun Ⓜ Clarke Quay

Prince of Wales (3, D3)

This Aussie-hewn pub has backpacker accommodation upstairs. Rub shoulders with resident surfy-looking beer-swillers effusing over acoustic rock on weeknights, and original bands on weekends.
☎ 6299 0130 🖵 www.pow.com.sg ✉ 101 Dunlop St 💲 free 🕓 from 9pm most nights Ⓜ Little India ♿ fair

Got a thing for Bryan Adams? Does Michael Bolton make your heart race? Singaporean nightlife is for you.

SPECTATOR SPORTS

Spectator sports in Singapore are limited by the heat and humidity, but you can always rely on the **Singapore Cricket Club** to roll the arm over, shout for a few LBWs and crack some cover drives across the Padang (p29).

For more on sport and fitness see p85.

Singapore Indoor Stadium (2, F4)

Most of Singapore's big-ticket sports and entertainment events – from international soccer to rock concerts, Disney on Ice and celebrity wrestling – are played out here; check the website or the *Straits Times* for details.

☎ 6348 5555 🖳 www.sis .gov.sg ✉ 2 Stadium Walk 💲 varies 🕓 box office 10am-10pm Mon-Sat, noon-8pm Sun Ⓜ Kallang then bus 11 ♿ good

Singapore Polo Club (2, E3)

Established in 1886, the SPC refuses to temper its 'Tally-ho old chap, into the fray!' approach to postcolonial life. Thank God! (...oh, and the Queen). Spectators are welcome at practice 'chukkas' through the week; international fixtures happen in May, September and October.

☎ 6854 3999 🖳 www.sing aporepoloclub.org ✉ 80 Mt Pleasant Rd 💲 free 🕓 5pm Tue, Thu, Sat & Sun Feb-Nov 🚌 54, 130, 162, 167, 980 ♿ fair

Singapore Turf Club (2, D2)

The tourist spiel claims 'It's more exiting with horses!'. We're not sure what 'it' entails, but the horse races sure are rousing. Seats range from grandstand ($3) up to Hibiscus Room ($20). Dress code is collared shirt and pants for men; closed shoes for women. Betting is government controlled. Giddyup.

☎ 6879 1000 🖳 www.turf club.com.sg ✉ 1 Turf Club Ave 💲 $3-20 🕓 6.30pm Fri, 2pm Sat, 2.30pm Sun Ⓜ Kranji ♿ fair

DANCE & CLASSICAL MUSIC

Chinese Theatre Circle (5, B2)

This Chinese opera company produces traditional operas in Chinese and English, resplendent in full costume and make-up. In addition to the major productions, Opera Karaoke (p30) and various cultural sessions also transpire.

☎ 6323 4862 🖳 www.ctc opera.com.sg ✉ 5 Smith St 💲 $20, incl dinner $35 🕓 box office noon-5pm

Tue-Thu, noon-5pm & 7-9pm Fri & Sat, 2-10pm Sun Ⓜ Chinatown

Singapore Chinese Orchestra (5, D3)

The SCO perform regular classical Chinese music concerts throughout the year; traditional instruments include the liuqin, ruan and sanxian. Free park and community centre performances also happen – check the website.

☎ 6440 3839 🖳 www .sco.com.sg ✉ Singapore Conference Hall, 7 Shenton Way 💲 varies Ⓜ Tanjong Pagar

Singapore Dance Theatre (3, C5)

Founded in 1988 the Singapore Dance Theatre produces traditional ballet favourites alongside contemporary works. Most performances happen at the Esplanade – Theatres on the Bay (p13). Don't miss July's Ballet Under the Stars season at Fort Canning ($19).

☎ 6338 0611 🖳 www .singaporedancetheatre.com ✉ 02 Fort Canning Centre, Cox Tce 💲 $28-68 Ⓜ Dhoby Ghaut

'Huzzah!'

Yet another lavish Chinese opera performance

Singapore Symphony Orchestra (3, D6)

This SSO plays at least once weekly at Victoria Concert Hall, the Botanic Gardens (p14) or the Esplanade – Theatres on the Bay (p13). Check the website for details; book in advance. Student and senior (age 60 plus) discounts available; leave kids under six years old with the nanny.

☎ 6348 5555 ☐ www.sso .org.sg ✉ Victoria Concert Hall, 11 Empress Pl $ $16-82 Ⓜ Raffles Place

GAY & LESBIAN SINGAPORE

The city's gay and lesbian scene revolves around Chinatown and the Tanjong Pagar area. Male homosexuality is illegal in Singapore; lesbianism doesn't officially exist! Crackdowns on venues are extremely rare, but they do happen. See p86 for more information.

Actors (3, C6)

Gay-friendly Actors is more like an effeminate version of *Cheers* than a raucous gay bar, but bartenders mete out vodka shooters and sympathy to the girls, guys, queers and straights as required. Expect a relaxed vibe, a 25-to-35 crowd, impromptu musical jams and the odd game of pool.

☎ 6533 2436 ✉ 02-13 South Bridge Rd $ free ⏰ 6pm-2am Mon-Sat Ⓜ Clarke Quay

Backstage Bar (5, B1)

The balcony at this cosy men's pub is a great spot to chat, flirt with local lads and otherwise play Rapunzel. Don't be put off by the 'PLU Members Only' sign downstairs – friends of the rainbow flag have automatic membership. The entrance is on Temple St.

☎ 6227 1712 ✉ 13A Trengganu St $ free ⏰ 7pm-2am Ⓜ Chinatown

Happy (5, B2)

Officialdom forbids kissing and taking your shirt off, but that doesn't seem to stop anyone. Happening Happy is mostly full of buff boys, but girls are welcome too. Indulge your inner 'Happysexual' (the signature cocktail) and shake your tush at the dawn.

☎ 6227 7400 ✉ 01-02/04, 21 Tanjong Pagar Rd $ $20 ⏰ 9pm-3am Mon-Sat Ⓜ Tanjong Pagar

Mox Bar & Café (5, B2)

More gay-friendly than out-and-out queer, Mox is a cool place to squeeze in a few heart-starters before wiggling downstairs to the effervescent Happy (left). The rooftop views are almost as interesting as the furniture, donated by people's grandmas.

☎ 6323 9438 ✉ 04-01, 21 Tanjong Pagar Rd $ free ⏰ 7pm-midnight Tue-Thu, 7pm-2am Fri & Sat Ⓜ Tanjong Pagar

Why Not? (5, B3)

Plant yourself on a podium and gyrate at one of Singapore's most popular backstreet G&L hangouts, playing nonstop house and crowd-pleaser anthems.

☎ 6323 3010 ✉ 58 Tras St $ free ⏰ 8pm-3am Mon-Thu, 10pm-3am Fri & Sat Ⓜ Tanjong Pagar

Xposé (5, C1)

It wasn't long ago that the concept of a regulation Singapore gay bar was too taboo to imagine, but that's exactly what Xposé is. Karaoke-phobes should stay away until after midnight when the mic shuts down, or run the gauntlet for the excellent Thai/Vietnamese dinner served here.

☎ 6323 2466 ✉ 208 South Bridge Rd $ free ⏰ 6pm-midnight Mon-Wed, 6pm-1am Thu & Sun, 6pm-2am Fri & Sat Ⓜ Chinatown ♿ Good

Sleeping

Orchard Rd groans under the weight of high-end chain hotel megaliths, while smaller, boutique midrange hotels in old shophouses convene around Chinatown. You won't be spoilt for choice, but there's a crop of excellent options for hardcore budgeters around Little India. Singapore has 8.94 million tourists annually and 84% hotel occupancy – book your bed in advance!

As usual, top-end hotels supply top-end facilities for top-end prices. Some rooms in shophouse hotels don't have windows and some don't have lifts; all hotels listed have air-conditioning.

In major hotels, a goods and services tax (GST), government tax and service charge are added to your bill – this is the 'plus-plus-plus' that follows the quoted price (eg $150+++), amounting to a tidy 16% on top of the room cost. 'Nett' means the price includes tax and a service charge. Hotels stipulate that you shouldn't tip when a service charge applies. GST and government taxes also apply in cheaper hotels but they're usually included in the quoted price.

Singapore's hotel industry is extremely competitive, with discounts of 25% to 50% common for longer stays, repeat visits, corporate deals and special promotions – it's worth asking!

ROOM RATES

Hotels are grouped according to published rates for a standard double room. But prices can be deceptive as discounts between 25% and 50% are common, especially if you book over the Internet; ask about special promotions when you book.

Deluxe	$400-650
Top End	$200-399
Midrange	$100-199
Budget	$40-99

Slumming it at Fullerton…we think not (opposite)

BOOK ACCOMMODATION ONLINE

For more accommodation reviews and recommendations by Lonely Planet authors, check out the online booking service at www.lonelyplanet.com. You'll find the true, insider lowdown on the best places to stay. Reviews are thorough and independent. Best of all, you can book online.

DELUXE

Four Seasons (4, B2)
The Four Seasons resides in quiet luxury a block behind the frenzy of Orchard Rd, its traditional Euro furnishings offset by Asiatic touches and an interesting art collection. Body buffs adore the air-conditioned tennis courts, fitness centre and swimming pools, while top-notch restaurants appease the gourmands. ☎ 6734 1110 ▯ www.fourseasons.com ✉ 190 Orchard Blvd Ⓜ Orchard Ⓖ excellent ✕ One-Ninety, Jiang-Nan Chun (p56)

Fullerton (3, D6)
This converted 1928 post office is one of *the* places to stay in Singapore. All rooms have broadband, minibar, safe, king-sized bed, spa, huge TV, honey-coloured marble bathrooms and uber-plush bathrobes. Standard rooms face the courtyard; suites have river views. It's pet-friendly, and the concierge is exceptional. Hard to beat! ☎ 6733 8388 ▯ www.fullertonhotel.com ✉ 1 Fullerton Sq Ⓜ Raffles Place Ⓖ good ♿ ✕ Post (p63)

Goodwood Park Hotel (4, C1)
Dating from 1900, this Rhineland-inspired remnant was here when tigers roamed Orchard Rd's plantations. Old-world opulence strays into uncool territory here and there (garish signs and naff pinkish-grey paint), but it's worth tolerating for the history whispering from the walls. Poolside suites are excellent. ☎ 6737 7411 ▯ www.goodwoodparkhotel.com.sg ✉ 22 Scotts Rd Ⓜ Orchard Ⓖ fair ♿ ✕ Gordon Grill (p56)

Raffles (3, D5)
Is it worth coughing up the cash to stay at Raffles? The rooms aren't as bright as modern hotels, but wooden floors, high ceilings, leafy verandas, unwavering colonial ambience and famous Sikh doorman more than compensate. Rooms start at $750, peaking out at $4500. Maybe you'll get Noel Coward's bed. ☎ 6337 1886 ▯ www.raffleshotel.com ✉ 1 Beach Rd Ⓜ City Hall Ⓖ good ✕ see p52

SENTOSA NIGHTS
If you feel like bunking down on Sentosa Island (p20) after a day basking on the beach, accommodation includes the sleek five-star **Sentosa Resort & Spa** (1, C2; ☎ 6275 0331; www.thesentosa.com.sg) and the wedding-cake cascades of the top-end **Shangri-La Rasa Sentosa Resort** (1, A1; ☎ 6275 0100; www.shangri-la.com). Also top-end is the charming, paint-peeling **Sijori Resort** (1, B2; ☎ 6271 2002; www.sijoriresort.com.sg), while the midrange **Costa Sands Resort** (1, B2; ☎ 6275 1034; www.costasands.com.sg) features shingle-roofed huts and a cliff-top pool. Zzzzz…

Get the olde-worlde feel at Goodwood Park Hotel

TOP END

Amara (3, B9)
The super-friendly, competent staff at Amara have a distinct absence of chips on their shoulders. From tasteful black-and-whites of old-time Singapore to the stone-walled swimming pool and Balinese spa, it's an unfailingly classy establishment, just far enough from the tourist trail.
☎ 6879 2555 ☐ www .amarahotels.com ✉ 165 Tanjong Pagar Rd Ⓜ Tanjong Pagar ♿ good 🍴 ✗ Thanying (☎ 6222 4688), Chinatown (p49)

Marriott (4, C2)
You can't miss the Marriott. It's the tall, angular one on the corner, with the silly hat. Selling points: location, business centre, gym, day spa, cosy (if dimly lit) rooms, and bathrooms with more marble than you're ever likely to see in one place. 'Poolside' views may require binoculars.
☎ 6735 5800 ☐ www .marriotthotels.com/sindt ✉ cnr Scotts & Orchard Rds Ⓜ Orchard ♿ good 🍴 ✗ Marriott Café, Orchard Rd (p56)

New Majestic Hotel (5, A2)
Oozing boutique sleek, the New Majestic has undergone an architectural overhaul, turning the old Majestic's 60 squishy rooms into 30 generous ones. Highlights include terrazzo lobby floors, hand-blown glass mobiles, private balconies and voyeuristic portals, looking up into the swimming pool, in the restaurant ceiling.
☎ 6511 4700 ☐ www .newmajestichotel.com

Marble, marble and more marble – the foyer of the Marriott

✉ 31-37 Bukit Pasoh Rd Ⓜ Outram Park ✗ Chinese restaurant, Chinatown (p49)

Scarlet (5, C2)
Wow! The Scarlet has seduced Singapore's boutique hotel market, leaving its competitors blushing. Occupying a string of gorgeous 1924 shophouses, 84 rooms are lustily decorated with deep velvet, gilt-framed mirrors, ebony timbers and plush Arabic cushions. *Sooooo* sexy! The rooftop bar, Breeze, is perfect for pre-dinner drinks.
☎ 6511 3333 ☐ www .thescarlethotel.com ✉ 33 Erskine Rd Ⓜ Chinatown, Tanjong Pagar ♿ fair ✗ Desire, Chinatown (p49)

Swissôtel The Stamford (3, D5)
Everyone raves about IM Pei's 2000-room Swissôtel, the tallest hotel in Southeast Asia. It boasts one of Singapore's hippest wining and dining complexes, the views are predictably sublime, and service standards are as elevated as the building.
☎ 6338 8585 ☐ www .swissotel-thestamford.com ✉ 2 Stamford Rd Ⓜ City Hall ♿ excellent 🍴 ✗ Equinox (p50)

MIDRANGE

Albert Court (3, D3)
At the southern ebb of Little India, this midrange winner is an immaculate, colonial-era hotel in a shophouse redevelopment that now shoots up eight storeys. Rooms have the usual mod cons, with a choice between fan and air-con. Promotional rates nudge budget levels.
☎ 6339 3939 ☐ www .albertcourt.com.sg ✉ 180 Albert St Ⓜ Little India ♿ good 🍴 ✗ Little India (p54)

Berjaya Hotel (5, B3)
This elegantly restored hotel in the heart of Chinatown offers small, plush rooms with just enough pomp and circumstance. Rooms overlooking the street have views; suites are two-storey. There's no swimming pool or gym but detailed colonial interiors and marble bathrooms will ease your disappointment.
☎ 6227 7678 ☐ www .berjayaresorts.com ✉ 83 Duxton Rd Ⓜ Tanjong Pagar ✗ L'Aigle d'Or (p49)

Gallery Hotel (3, A6)
Singapore's first boutique hotel is still totally hip.

Rooms feature retro furnishings, zanily coloured linen, low-volt track lighting, frosted-glass bathroom walls and room numbers branded into the floorboards; even standard-category rooms are spacious. The glass rooftop pool and free Internet are bonuses.

☎ 6849 8686 ⌨ www .galleryhotel.com.sg ✉ 76 Robertson Quay Ⓜ Clarke Quay 🚌 33, 54, 139, 195 ♿ good ♿ ✕ Clarke Quay (p58)

Hotel 1929 (5, A2)

The architects have maximised limited space at Singapore's grooviest boutique hotel, the small but cheery rooms finished with vintage designer chairs and technicolour mosaics. Book ahead for a rooftop suite with private terrace and outdoor claw-foot bath.

☎ 6347 1929 ⌨ www .hotel1929.com ✉ 50 Keong Saik Rd Ⓜ Outram Park ♿ ✕ Ember (p49)

Inn at Temple Street (5, B1)

Nondescript, uninspiring, run-of-the-mill… All terms you could easily bandy about these quarters, but sometimes in life you just need something solid to lean on. Clean, safe, good-value, reliable accommodation in a top Chinatown location.

☎ 6221 5333 ⌨ www .theinn.com.sg ✉ 36 Temple St Ⓜ Chinatown ♿ ✕ Chinatown (p49)

Robertson Quay Hotel (3, B5)

Probably the best-value hotel along the river, this chubby circular tower has immaculate rooms and a potted-palm rooftop swimming pool. Pros: location, location, location; cons: unadventurous interiors and Clemenceau Ave traffic. Internet discounts are often available.

☎ 6735 3333 ⌨ www .robertsonquayhotel.com.sg ✉ 15 Merbau Rd Ⓜ Clarke Quay 🚌 33, 54, 139, 195

♿ ✕ Clarke Quay, Robertson Quay (p58)

Royal Peacock (5, A2)

Beautiful lobby, beautiful staff and a fantastic shophouse location amongst the Keong Saik Rd hubbub. Rooms are painted with a rich peacock palette and have character by the bucket-load; cheaper rooms are sans windows, and a little cramped. Prices are sometimes slashed to budget level.

☎ 6223 3522 ⌨ www.roy alpeacockhotel.com ✉ 55 Keong Saik Rd Ⓜ Outram Park ♿ ✕ Chinatown (p49)

Sha Villa (4, F3)

Just around the corner from the towering bustle of Orchard Rd, this 40-room colonial white elephant has endured while neighbouring relics have tasted the wrecking ball. Timber-floored rooms are evocatively furnished, even the smallest seem more cute than poky. Standard rooms have

No jumping on the beds at Royal Peacock

generous bathrooms but no windows.

☎ 6734 7117 ⌨ www.sha .org.sg ✉ 64 Lloyd Rd Ⓜ Somerset ♿ fair ✗ Rosette, Orchard Rd (p56)

Strand Hotel (3, C4)

Some effort and imagination has gone into elevating the Strand above your average midranger. Rooms are decorated with earthy colours, jungle-print fabrics and ballet-dancer door numbers. There's a pool table on the terrace and no-fuss, un-obsequious service.

☎ 6388 1866 ⌨ www .strandhotel.com.sg ✉ 25 Bencoolen St Ⓜ Dhoby Ghaut ⚱ ✗ on-site café, Colonial District (p50)

BUDGET

Hangout @ Mt Emily (3, C3)

This sleek boutique hostel nestles between Orchard Rd and Little India in Mt Emily's leafy glades. Dorms and private rooms are immaculate, and there's a sensational rooftop terrace, library, café, free Internet and cosy lounge areas. Vibrant colours are splashed across walls; murals are by local art students.

☎ 6438 5588 ⌨ www .hangouthotels.com ✉ 10A Upper Wilkie Rd Ⓜ Little India ♿ fair ⚱ ✗ Little India (p54)

InnCrowd (3, D3)

There's no excuse for neglecting your inner party-animal here, with the cheapest beer in town! What they lose on lager they recoup on accommodation, with dozens of fresh-faced dorm-dwellers

sardined into the loft. The atmosphere's convivial, with helpful staff, bike hire and a dedicated party room around the corner.

☎ 6296 9169 ⌨ www .the-inncrowd.com ✉ 73 Dunlop St Ⓜ Little India ✗ Little India (p54)

Lloyd's Inn (4, F3)

Surrounded by crumbling mansions just off Orchard Rd, this strange, weathered 1940s building seems to have been perversely designed to minimise natural light and access to the adjoining garden. Rooms are tidy and good value; some on the 2nd floor have garden views.

☎ 6737 7309 ⌨ www .lloydinn.com ✉ 2 Lloyd Rd Ⓜ Somerset ✗ Orchard Rd (p56)

New 7th Storey (3, E4)

An urban planning aberration, the New 7th Storey

Hotel stands in gothic isolation in the middle of a park, as if all the buildings around it somehow vanished. It's a well-run, friendly place with clean dorms and good-value doubles. How long will it evade developers' clutches?

☎ 6337 0251 ⌨ www.nss hotel.com ✉ 229 Rochor Rd Ⓜ Bugis ✗ Colonial District (p50)

Sleepy Sam's (3, E3)

It's not often you'd list a backpacker hostel as a 'must stay', but Sleepy Sam's qualifies. It's more like a boutique hotel than a hostel – dark-wood Asian furnishings, deep ochre colours, screened-off bunks, cushion-strewn DVD area, great staff and fabulous location in the shadows of the Sultan Mosque. Brilliant!

☎ 9277 4988 ⌨ www .sleepysams.com ✉ 55 Bussorah St Ⓜ Bugis ✗ Kampong Glam (p54)

Save up for a drink at Raffles (p71)

About Singapore

HISTORY

Malay legend tells of a Sumatran prince sheltering from a storm on the island of Temasek and spotting a lion – a good omen prompting the prince to found a city there called Singapura (Lion City). Actual records of Singapore's early history are sketchy – originally it was an insignificant port squeezed between muscular neighbours Sumatra and Melaka. Singapore's official history begins in 1819 with the arrival of Sir Stamford Raffles, who was declared Singapore's founder in the 1970s in order to 'neutrally' settle rival claims by local Malays and Chinese.

SIR STAMFORD RAFFLES

Raffles – cultural scholar, Singaporean colonist, naturalist and founder of the London Zoo – died aged 45 from a probable brain tumour after suffering extended bouts of fierce, incapacitating headaches. Having fallen out with the East India Company, his death was ignored by London society, but many years later on the other side of the globe, Singapore marked the 175th anniversary of Raffles' landing with unprecedented celebrations. These days it's hard to go anywhere in Singapore without bumping into the words 'Stamford' or 'Raffles' along the way.

Colonial Conquest

In the late 18th century Britain began looking for a harbour in the Strait of Melaka that would usurp its Portuguese and Dutch competitors and secure its trade lines between China, India and the Malay world.

Young Stamford Raffles arrived in Singapore in 1819 to find the Johor empire divided, with two contenders for the sultanship. The Dutch favoured one candidate, so Raffles backed rival contender Hussein and proclaimed him sultan, clinching the deal by signing a treaty with an eminent *temenggong* (senior judge). This exchange ended with the 1824 cash buyout of Hussein and the judge, transferring Singapore's ownership to the British East India Company. Among other things, it was Raffles' idea to divide the city into ethnic neighbourhoods.

Early Days

Singapore was soon teeming with Chinese immigrants, the Brits forging good trading relations with the Straits-born Chinese-Malays, or Peranakans, who found an identity in the Union Jack, British law and citizenship. Difficult early years were marred by bad sanitation, disease, British Empire–sponsored opium addiction, and

Exhibit at Images of Singapore (p20)

piracy. In 1887, interracial tensions led to riots.

By the 1930s and early 1940s, politics dominated the intellectual scene, the Indian independence movement and communist struggles in China capturing Singapore's imagination. Singaporeans vehemently opposed Japan's invasions of China in 1931 and 1937.

WWII & the Japanese Invasion

The Singaporean Chinese were to pay a heavy price for opposing Japanese imperialism when General Yamashita Tomoyuki pushed his thinly stretched army into the undefended northwest of Singapore on 15 February 1942. For the British, who had established a vital naval base near the city in the 1920s, surrender was sudden and humiliating, and 140,000 Australian, New Zealand, British and oft-overlooked Indian, Dutch and Malay troops were killed or imprisoned.

Japanese rule was harsh in Singapore, temporarily renamed Syonan (Light of the South). Yamashita herded up and interned Europeans, many in the infamous Changi prison. Thousands of Chinese (Singapore claims 50,000; Japan says 6000) were targeted for torture and mass execution at Sentosa and Changi Beach. Malays and Indians were subject to systematic abuse. Inflation skyrocketed; food, medicines and other essentials became scarce; and starvation ensued.

When the war ended with the atomic bombing of Nagasaki and Japan's surrender on 14 August 1945, Singapore was passed back into British control. Despite an official apology in 1991 and generous monetary loans, Singapore has never forgotten, or forgiven, the Japanese.

Post-War Alienation

The British were welcomed back to Singapore but their right (and ability) to rule was now in question. Post-war poverty, unemployment and nationalist sentiment provided a groundswell of support for communism, and Singapore moved slowly towards self-government.

By the early 1950s the 'communist threat' had waned but left-wing activity was still on the upswing. One of the rising stars of this era was Lee Kuan Yew, a third-generation Straits-born Chinese who had studied law at Cambridge. The socialist People's Action Party (PAP) was founded in 1954 with Lee as secretary-general.

Under arrangements for internal self-government, PAP won a majority of seats in the new Legislative Assembly in 1959, and Lee Kuan Yew became the first Singaporean prime minister – a title he held for the next 31 years.

Japanese uniform on display at Changi Museum & Chapel (p22)

Singapore's MRT Expo Station

Independent Singapore

By the early 1960s Britain devised a way to withdraw regional colonial rule by creating the new state of Malaysia, uniting Malaya with Sabah, Sarawak and Singapore. In 1965 Singapore was expelled, largely due to Malay fears of Chinese dominance. Singapore reluctantly struck out on its own and vigorously survived. Despite having no natural resources, under Lee Kuan Yew it quickly entrenched itself as Asia's financial centre and an 'economic miracle'. Today, under Prime Minister Lee Hsien Loong (Lee Kuan Yew's oldest son), Singapore is rapidly developing itself as an IT, transport, ideas and cultural hub.

ENVIRONMENT

Singapore stands out as an environmentally enlightened country in the region, although environmental groups say its land reclamation projects are destroying the environment of the surrounding islands. Recycling is increasingly accepted, while strict punitive laws control littering and waste emissions. Development has left little of Singapore's wilderness intact, but growing ecological interest and public desire for green space is urging the government towards conservation. Pockets of primary and secondary rainforest survive around Bukit Timah Nature Reserve (p19), with mangroves on the north coast and offshore islands.

Singapore has a terrific Mass Rapid Transit (MRT) rail system and an extensive bus network. Good public transport, $90,000 Hyundais and government car ownership restrictions equals remarkably pollution-free air. Like most countries, Singapore wants to conserve its environment but not at the expense of economic growth and prosperity.

LEE KUAN YEW

Under Lee's 31-year paternal reign, Singapore pursued an ambitious and highly successful programme of defence, health, education, pension and housing schemes. Meanwhile political stability was ensured by exiling or jailing dissidents, banning critical publications and controlling public speech. In 1990 Lee Kuan Yew resigned in style but remains influential as 'Minister Mentor', issuing advice on everything from protocol to diet. You can't question his patriotism. 'Even from my sickbed,' said Lee in 1988, 'even if you are going to lower me into the grave and I feel that something is wrong, I'll get up.'

GOVERNMENT & POLITICS

In theory, Singapore has a democratically elected government based on the Westminster system. In practice, electoral laws are biased towards the ruling People's Action Party (PAP), which has been in power since independence. The unicameral parliament has 84 elected members representing 52 electoral divisions. Voting is compulsory. Governments are elected for five years, but a ruling government can dissolve parliament and call an election at any time. In the May 2006 parliamentary election, the PAP won a landslide 82 seats, though the percentage of votes won was 66.6%, down from 73.3% in 2001.

The PAP argues that since it listens to all opposition and is happy to adopt good ideas, there is no need for political plurality. As well as having elected members, the government can appoint an opposition if fewer than four opposition members are elected. Singapore also has a popularly elected president, SR Nathan, but the position is largely ceremonial.

The legal system is also based on the British system, with the Supreme Court as the ultimate arbitrator. The judiciary's independence is enshrined in the constitution, but many judges are appointed on short tenure, their renewal subject to party approval. Rulings against the government have resulted in new laws rushed through parliament to ensure government victory.

Outspoken political opposition candidates are silenced by crippling defamation suits, jail sentences or being found guilty of 'tax evasion'.

> **JUST THE FACTS MA'AM**
> - Singapore has as a teensy surface area of 683 sq km.
> - In a population of 4.43 million, overseas workers number 450,000.
> - Singapore averages around one execution every nine days.
> - The country's official languages are Malay, Mandarin, Tamil and English.
> - Lee Kuan Yew nominated the air-conditioner as the most influential invention of the 20th century.
> - Air-conditioners account for one-third of Singapore's electricity usage.
> - Singapore's port is the third busiest in the world.
> - Tourists shell out $10.8 billion in Singapore every year, $1 billion of this on accommodation.

ECONOMY

Singapore has no natural resources other than its harbour and well-educated population. Despite this and its diminutive size, the country has become Southeast Asia's economic boomtown. Prosperity has come courtesy of its international trade-crossroads location, the promotion of free trade, and the country's attractiveness to foreign investors (with generous tax breaks, few restrictions on the exchange of currency and excellent infrastructure).

Singapore's growth rate averaged around 9% for the first 30 years of independence. The late-'90s Asian financial crisis and a recession from 2001 to 2003 put the brakes on, then the outbreak of SARS (severe acute respiratory syndrome) gave the country a huge scare – tourist arrivals and consumer spending plummeted.

Things are sailing along on even economic keel these days. Manufacturing, for so long the engine room of Singapore's success, is in decline, due in large part to the rapid growth of China and India. The government is trying to remodel the economy and build up sectors such as biomedical engineering and multimedia to ensure the country's future. Massive tourism investments are also in the pipeline.

'Be Spontaneous' – read a newspaper

SOCIETY & CULTURE

Outsiders often portray Singapore as a soulless money-making machine – an unkind assessment, though not without basis. As prosperous Singapore forges into the 21st century, the government is keen to define Singaporean identity and promote Asian values. Neo-Confucian ideals based on family subservience, societal decency, hard work and the desire to succeed dovetail neatly into authoritarian government notions of 'Asian democracy', which argue that Western pluralism is a luxury Singapore can't afford. Unlike neighbouring Malaysia, Singapore promotes multiculturalism – economic success and the government's power monopoly depend on stable interracial relations (however, in general class terms the Chinese dominate the upper echelons while Malays and Indians lag behind).

Singaporeans enjoy good education, health care and government-owned housing. In return they endure a barrage of government campaigns attempting to create conformity and cohesion at all costs. Programmes range from 'Be Spontaneous' campaigns to fines for not flushing public toilets, government-sponsored dating programmes (to promote procreation), the Filial Piety law that allows parents to sue their kids for upkeep, and tax breaks for well-educated mothers (ie tertiary-educated women).

Freedom of speech and the press is limited and publicly critiquing the government – even at Speakers' Corner (p29)! – can land you behind bars. Censorship is a sensitive issue, especially given current attempts to promote Singapore as an arts city. Despite Singapore's vibrant queer scene, homosexuality is still illegal, gay sex punishable by a 10-year jail sentence. In 2003 the government made international news when it 'quietly' changed

BABA & NONYA

Singapore's Padang-promenading colonists found friends among the Peranakan community – local families whose distinct culture combined Chinese and Malay traditions. Peranakan women are known as Nonya, the men as Baba – you'll see these names used in some of the city's traditional Peranakan restaurants. 'Peranakan', which means 'half-caste', wasn't always a flattering term but today Singapore's museums pay nostalgic homage to this ethnic group.

> ## THE SINGAPORE SNORT
> Woah, what the *hell* was that!? You'll be standing on the MRT or in a coffee queue when someone behind you will spontaneously erupt with an almighty, earth-shattering snort, collecting mucous from the nasal passages and depositing it somewhere far below with an audible swallow. The first time you hear it you'll fear for your life, but don't worry, it's habitual amongst Singaporean men (women never snort!). A physiological response to the government's anti-spitting laws perhaps?

policy to allow gays to work in government jobs – but the law criminalising homosexuality would remain unchanged (confusing huh?).

Perhaps Singapore's greatest contemporary challenge is to convince its youth – many of whom have enjoyed a lifetime of relative financial security – that all these restrictions are for the greater good.

Etiquette

Singapore's dress code could be described as 'smart casual' – the only shabby looking people you'll see are Western backpackers fresh in from Ko Pha Ngan. Businesspeople wear suits.

When exchanging business cards offer yours humbly, name-side up, pinching the card between both thumbs. Act like you're thoroughly absorbing the details of received cards even if you're not, and don't put them away before the offeree does.

Maintaining face is important in Singapore as elsewhere in Asia – smile and remain calm in disputes, and never lose your temper.

Religion plays a major role in people's lives, so treat it and devotees with maximum respect. At temples and shrines, dress modestly and remove your shoes. Feet are considered unclean, so avoid pointing your foot at people and at deities at temples.

Passionate public kissing is frowned upon, but handholding is accepted; it's OK for Indian and Bangladeshi foreign workers to hold hands with their male buddies (see p17).

Offerings at Sri Mariamman Temple (p17)

ARTS

Having proved itself an economic powerhouse, Singapore now wants to be seen as a creative nation. Singapore hosts numerous arts festivals throughout the year, the Esplanade – Theatres on the Bay (p13) arts complex elevating the arts to big-business status.

Local bands don't attract much attention, but both theatre and the visual arts are burgeoning and dominate the contemporary arts scene, driven mainly by young Chinese intellectuals. Galleries (p24) open and close with regularity, but the scene remains vibrant, painting, sculpture and multimedia the vehicles of choice for explorations into the tensions between Western art practices and the perceived erosion of traditional values.

Noted Singaporean artisans include writer/artist Swie Hian Tan, sculptor Han Sai Por, theatre director Ivan Heng, and actor, writer and director Alvin Tan. Local pop-culture gurus include columnist, musician and DJ X'Ho, and hip-hop artist Sheikh Haikel.

Singapore Art Museum (p23)

Chinese Opera

Chinese opera has its vaudevillian roots in Cantonese tradition. What it lacks in literary nuance it makes up for with garish costumes and crashing music. Performances can last entire evenings; it's usually easy to get the gist of things. Street and housing-block performances are held during festivals such as Chinese New Year (January/February), the Festival of the Hungry Ghosts (p61) and the Festival of the Nine Emperor Gods (October/November).

SPEAK GOOD SINGLISH

The Singaporean government regularly runs 'Speak Good English' campaigns, actively discouraging 'Singlish' in TV and radio shows. But Singaporeans continue to revel in their local vernacular, a unique (and often very funny) mix of English – cut, clipped, reversed and revamped – Malay and Hokkien Chinese. Common Singlish-isms include: *ah beng* (unsophisticated, uneducated person with no fashion sense or style, who tends to believe social status depends on conspicuous accessories and who isn't nearly as cool as he thinks); *ang mo* (foreigner); *Can?* (Is that OK?); *Can!* (No problemo, that's cool with me!); and *lah* (added to the end of sentences for emphasis). For some colourful examples of Singlish, see the Coxford Singlish Dictionary at www.talkingcock.com.

Film

The annual **Singapore Film Festival** (www.filmfest.org.sg) is bolstering Singaporeans' taste for fine film. In 1998 the Singapore Film Commission was established to 'nurture, support and promote' Singaporean talent in the film industry; a 'Mature 18' rating was introduced to overcome scissor-happy government censorship. Notable Singaporean films include Eric Khoo's *Mee Pok Man* and *12 Storeys*, a gritty depiction of HDB life; Tay Teck Lock's *Money No Enough*; and Glen Goei's disco hit *Forever Fever*. Other favourites are *Army Daze*, a military comedy; *I Not Stupid* and *I Not Stupid Too*, incredibly popular tragicomedies about non-conformity in Singapore's schools; the satire *Talking Cock*; and Royston Tan's award-winning short film *15*.

Directory

Flights, tours and rail tickets can be booked online at www.lonelyplanet.com/travel_services.

ARRIVAL & DEPARTURE
Air
CHANGI INTERNATIONAL AIRPORT
Singapore's slick, squeaky-clean **Changi International Airport** (2, J3) is about 20km east of the city centre. It has two terminals, with a third due for completion in 2008. Most airlines operate from Terminal 1, a handful (including Singapore Airlines) from Terminal 2. Changi's facilities include a 24-hour medical centre, post office, free showers, Internet access and local phone calls, left luggage (p83), children's playground and free city tours for transit passengers. For details check out www.changi.airport.com.sg, the information brochures or airport magazine distributed throughout the airport or ask at the information counter.

Information
Some useful numbers:
General inquiries (☎ 6541 2267)
Customer service (☎ 6542 1122)
Flight information (☎ 1800 542 4422)
Hotel booking service (☎ Terminal 1 6542 6966, Terminal 2 ☎ 6545 9789)

CLIMATE CHANGE & TRAVEL
Travel – especially air travel – is a significant contributor to global climate change. At Lonely Planet, we believe that all travellers have a responsibility to limit their personal impact. As a result, we have teamed with Rough Guides and other concerned industry partners to support Climatecare.org, which allows travellers to offset the greenhouse gases they are responsible for with contributions to sustainable travel schemes. Lonely Planet offsets all staff and author travel. For more information, check out www.lonely planet.com.

Airport Access
Taxi or the MRT (Mass Rapid Transit) are the best ways to reach the city. MRT trains depart Changi for the CBD from 5.30am to 11.18pm ($2.50, 30 minutes, every 12 minutes). Trains to Changi from City Hall Station run from 6am to midnight. In both directions, you'll probably need to change trains at Tanah Merah Station (nothing complex – just cross the platform).

Shuttle buses to the CBD and most hotels leave every 30 minutes from 6am to 6pm and every 15 minutes from 6.05pm to midnight (tickets $7/5). Book and pay at the counter in the arrival hall.

Taxis to the city cost around $20, plus a surcharge. From Friday to Sunday the surcharge is $5 from 5pm to midnight and 50% of the fare from midnight to 6am; at all other times the surcharge is $3. Alternatively, you can hire a limo taxi to your hotel for $30.

Bus
Air-con express depart for and arrive from neighbouring Malaysia and Thailand around-the-clock. Buses to both countries depart from the Golden Mile Complex (3, F3) on Beach Rd, with buses to Malaysia also departing the Queen St Bus Terminal (3, E3) and Lavender St Bus Terminal (3, F1).

Call the following numbers directly for details, or consult the Singapore Tourist Bureau (p89):
Singapore–Johor Bahru (☎ 1800 287 2727)
Singapore–Kuala Lumpur (☎ 6292 8254)
Singapore–Malacca (☎ 6293 5915)
Singapore–Thailand (☎ 6293 6692)

Train
From Singapore there are three air-conditioned express trains daily to Malaysia (about seven hours to Kuala Lumpur) with continuing services to Thailand. Contact **Keretapi Tanah Melayu** (KTM; ☎ 6222 5165; www.ktmb.com.my) or its booking office at

the **Singapore Railway Station** (3, A9; ☎ 6222 5165; Keppel Rd) for information. Depending on the carriage class and whether you ride in a seat or a sleeper, a Kuala Lumpur fare will be between $30 and $110.

The luxurious antique **Eastern & Oriental Express** (☎ 6392 3500; www.orient-express.com) trundles north from Singapore to Kuala Lumpur, Butterworth, Bangkok, Chiang Mai and Angkor Wat. Fares veer dramatically from $600 to $6000.

Ferry

Ferry services depart daily from the **HarbourFront Ferry Terminal** (1, B1; ☎ 6270 2228) and **Tanah Merah Ferry Terminal** (2, J4; ☎ 6542 4369), chugging out to neighbouring Indonesian islands Pulau Batam and Pulau Bintan respectively. Return fares are around $30 to Batam; $40 to Bintan.

Ferries depart from the **Changi Ferry Terminal** (2, J3; ☎ 6546 8518) and **Changi Point Ferry Terminal** (2, J2; ☎ 6542 7944) daily for Tanjong Belungkor (return $22) and Pengerang (return $14) respectively, in Malaysia.

Travel Documents
PASSPORT & VISA

Travellers from the USA, UK, Australia, NZ, Canada, South Africa and most European countries automatically receive a 30-day tourist visa on entry if arriving by air, or a 14-day visa if arriving by land or sea. Passports must be valid for at least six months from the entry date, and you may be asked to produce a return/onwards plane ticket and evidence of a healthy bank account. For visa extensions, the **Immigration & Checkpoints Authority** (3, F2; ☎ 6391 6100; 10 Kallang Rd) bamboozles you with forms, queues, red tape and bureaucracy. Applications take at least a day to process.

Customs & Duty Free

Drugs (don't even think about it), guns, firecrackers and pornography are strictly forbidden, but bring as much cash as you like! Take a letter from your doctor if you carry prescription medication.

Visitors are allowed to bring in 1L of duty free wine, beer or spirits providing they're over 18 years old, aren't arriving from Malaysia or Indonesia and have been away from Singapore for at least 48 hours.

Left Luggage

Left luggage facilities are available at Changi Airport for between $3.15 and $8.40 per day depending on the item's size. There are counters at Terminal 1 (☎ 6214 0628) and Terminal 2 (☎ 6214 1683). Alternatively, if you've been staying with them, most hotels will let you leave your bags with them if you're killing time waiting for a flight.

GETTING AROUND

Singapore has fantastic public transport, a tangled web of bus and MRT train routes taking you to the doorstep of most sights. The MRT is easy to navigate, but stops are sometimes far apart (walking in 35°C humidity is sweaty work!). The new Circle Line is due to open in 2008. Pick up a free MRT system map at any MRT station, and the *Bus Guide & Bus Stop Directory* ($3.90) from bookshops. Due to car ownership limitations, taxis are also considered public transport.

In this book, the nearest MRT stations and/or bus numbers are listed after the Ⓜ and 🚌 icons.

Travel Passes

An ez-link card from any MRT station allows you to travel by train and bus; swipe the card over sensors as you enter and leave a station or bus. Cards cost $15: $7 worth of travel, a $5 nonrefundable charge and a $3 refundable deposit redeemable when you return the card. You can top-up cards at ATM-style machines at stations.

If you've only got a day in Singapore, pick up a free Transit Day Pass from the Singapore Visitors Centre in the Transit Hall at

Changi Airport (after clearing immigration), which gives you 10 free rides on the MRT within 24 hours.

MRT

The ultra-clean, safe and efficient Singapore **MRT** (☎ 1800 336 8900; www.smrt .com.sg) subway and light-rail system is the most comfortable and hassle-free way to get around. Trains run from around 5.30am to midnight, departing every three to four minutes at peak times and every six to eight off-peak. Fares range from 70¢ to $3, and are cheaper if you use an ez-link card (see Travel Passes, p83).

Bus

Singapore's bus service should be the envy of the world. You rarely have to wait more than a few minutes for a bus, and they'll take you almost anywhere. Some even have TVs to entertain passengers!

Fares range from 60¢ to $1.50; there are also a few flat-rate buses. When you board the bus, drop the exact money into the fare box (no change is given) or swipe your ez-link card (see Travel Passes, p83). For inquiries contact **SBS Transit** (☎ 1800 287 2727; www.sbstransit.com.sg).

TOURIST BUSES

The following tourist bus services loop between Orchard Rd, Chinatown, the Colonial District and Little India.

CityBuzz (☎ 1800 225 5663; www.city buzz.com.sg) runs double-decker buses on loops of the main city areas every 10 to 15 minutes between 10am and 10pm, stopping at key attractions. Day passes ($5) are available from drivers, Singapore Visitors Centres and authorised agents.

Singapore Airlines runs the **SIA Hop-On** (☎ 9457 2965; www.asiatours.com.sg/sia .htm) tourist bus, traversing the main tourist arteries every 30 minutes daily from 9am to 6pm. Tickets are available from the driver: $8 for a day pass; $3 with a Singapore Airlines or SilkAir boarding pass or ticket.

The **Singapore Trolley** (☎ 6339 6833; www.singaporeexplorer.com.sg/trolley .htm), a bus not-so-cunningly disguised as an old-fashioned tram, circles the major tourist areas between 9.40am and 4.55pm. All-day tickets from the driver cost $9/7.

Taxi

Taxis swarm like locusts except when changing shift between 4pm and 5pm, when it's raining and between 10pm and 11pm, when they can be impossible to find. Taxis are metered and cost around $2.40 for the first kilometre, then 10¢ for each additional 220m. The average journey costs between $5 and $10, plus surcharges for phone and advance booking, peak travel to the CBD, and from the airport. Credit-card payments incur a 10% surcharge. If you order a cab by phone you'll be asked your name and destination; a message then tells you the licence plate of your cab. Taxi companies include the following:

City Cab (☎ cash bookings 6552 2222, credit card 6553 8888)

Comfort CabLink (☎ 6552 1111)

SMRT Cabs (☎ 6555 8888)

Car & Motorcycle

On a short Singapore stay you're unlikely to need your own wheels. Most locals don't have cars, and CBD driving and parking restrictions can turn a cruisy drive into a living hell. If you do need to hire a car, the following companies have branches at Changi Airport and as listed below:

Avis (3, A6; ☎ 6737 1668; www.avis.com .sg; 01-17 392 Havelock Rd)

Budget (3, D7; ☎ 6532 3948; www .budget.com; 26-01A Clifford Centre, 24 Raffles Pl)

Hertz (4, C1; ☎ 1800 734 46646; www .hertz.com; 01-01 15 Scotts Rd)

PRACTICALITIES
Business Hours

Government office hours are generally 9am to 6pm Monday to Friday, and 10am to 1pm on Saturday (see also Opening Hours, p88).

Climate & When to Go

Singapore is right on the Equator, and it's damn humid. The wet season is technically from November to January, but temperature and rainfall are fairly steady year-round – visit anytime!

If you can, align your visit with one of Singapore's festivals. Chinese New Year (January/February), Thaipusam (January) and the Festival of the Hungry Ghosts (August/September) are among the more spectacular. The Singapore Food Festival and the Great Singapore Sale happen in July. See also p61.

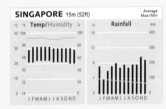

Disabled Travellers

You'll find most major hotels, shopping malls and tourist attractions have good wheelchair access, but Little India's and Chinatown's crowded narrow footpaths will challenge anyone with mobility, sight or hearing issues. Taxis are plentiful, the MRT is wheelchair-friendly and Singaporeans are happy to help out. We've used the disabled icon ♿ to indicate venues with disabled access, which are rated as 'excellent', 'good' or 'fair'.

Access Singapore (www.dpa.org.sg) is a useful guidebook for the disabled; it's available from the website and STB offices (see p89).

Discounts

Children receive up to 50% discounts at most tourist venues, sometimes gauged by how tall they are rather than age. They can ride the MRT for free if they're under 90cm tall. Students with ID cards receive discounts at some venues.

Electricity

Electricity supply is reliable and runs at 220V to 240V and 50 cycles. Plugs are of the three-pronged, square-pin type used in the UK.

Embassies & Consulates

Foreign consulates and embassies in Singapore include the following:

Australia (2, E4; ☎ 6836 4100; www .australia.org.sg; 25 Napier Rd)

Canada (3, C7; ☎ 6854 5900; www .dfait-maeci.gc.ca/asia/singapore; 11-01 1 George St)

New Zealand (4, D2; ☎ 6235 9966; www.nzembassy.com/singapore; 15-06 Ngee Ann City, Tower A, 391A Orchard Rd)

South Africa (3, D5; ☎ 6339 3319; www .dfa.gov.za/webmissions; 15-01/06 Odeon Towers, 331 North Bridge Rd)

UK (2, E4; ☎ 6424 4200; www.britishhigh commission.gov.uk; 100 Tanglin Rd)

USA (2, E4; ☎ 6476 9100; http://singa pore.usembassy.gov; 27 Napier Rd)

Emergency

Heavy penalties mean Singapore has a low crime rate – both sexes can feel comfortable walking around at night. Pickpockets sometimes target tourists and the odd gang fight makes front-page news, but unless you go looking for it, trouble is unlikely to come looking for you. Don't import, take or sell drugs in Singapore or hang out with anyone who does – the death penalty awaits...

Ambulance/Fire (☎ 995)

Police (☎ 999)

SOS Helpline (☎ 1800 774 5935)

Fitness
GOLF

Golf is big business in Singapore, and big status too. Most clubs are members-only, but the following courses will let you tee-off for $20 to $40 for nine holes on weekdays, $30 to $50 on weekends:

Executive Golf Course (2, E2; ☎ 6556 0600; Upper Seletar Reservoir, Track 7 Mandai Rd)

Green Fairways (2, D3; ☎ 6468 7233; 60 Fairways Dr)
Seletar Base Golf Course (2, F2; ☎ 6481 4745; 244 Oxford St, Seletar Base)
Tanglin Golf Course (2, E4; ☎ 6473 7236; 130E Minden Rd)

GYMS

Most big hotels have gyms, or gym junkies can head to **Fitness First** (4, D2; ☎ 6737 7889; 05-01 Paragon, 290 Orchard Rd; per session $40; ☷ 6.30am-10.30pm Mon-Sat, 8am-10pm Sun). See also the Amrita Spa (p31).

SWIMMING

At $1.30/1 and open from 8am to 9.30pm, Singapore's 50m public swimming pools are winners:
Delta Swimming Complex (2, E4; ☎ 6474 7573; 900 Tiong Bahru Rd)
Jalan Besar Swimming Complex (3, E2; ☎ 6293 9058; 100 Tyrwhitt Rd)
Katong Swimming Complex (2, G4; ☎ 6344 9609; 111 Wilkinson Rd)
Serangoon Swimming Complex (2, F3; ☎ 6288 4606; 35A Yio Chu Kang Rd)

YOGA

Shambhala Yoga Centre (4, B2; ☎ 6735 2163; www.comoshambhala.bz; 06-05 Forum, 583 Orchard Rd; 1½-hr class $28; ☷ 9am-9pm Mon-Fri, 9.30am-5pm Sat & Sun) has Hatha, Iyengar, Vinyasa and Ashtanga classes, and Pilates.

Gay & Lesbian Travellers

Homosexuality is illegal in Singapore – penalties range from 10 years to life for engaging in homosexual sex – but authorities generally turn a blind eye to the queer scene. See p69 for venues, and check out www.utopia-asia.com, www.fridae.com and www.sgboy.com.

Singaporeans are conservative about displays of public affection; women and Indian and Bangladeshi foreign workers can get away with same-sex hand holding,

but an overtly gay couple doing the same would attract attention. That said, vocal or aggressive homophobia is unlikely to rear it's ugly head.

Health
IMMUNISATIONS

Check with your doctor regarding immunisation requirements (your doctor may suggest Hepatitis A shots). Visitors arriving within six days from areas where yellow fever is endemic (Africa, South America) will have to produce a vaccination certificate or submit to a health screening.

PRECAUTIONS

You can drink tap water everywhere in Singapore except Pulau Ubin. Singapore is hot and humid, so keep your fluids up (no, not beer). Sunburn can sneak up on you too, even when it's cloudy, so cover up. Avoid pre-prepared hawker centre food – go for something woked on the spot! There have been recent dengue fever outbreaks in the city – use mosquito repellent when outside.

MEDICAL SERVICES

Hospitals with 24-hour accident and emergency departments:
Gleneagles Hospital (2, E4; ☎ 6470 5688; 6A Napier Rd)
Mount Elizabeth Hospital (4, D1; ☎ 6731 2218; 3 Mt Elizabeth Rd)
Raffles Hospital (3, E3; ☎ 6311 1111; 585 North Bridge Rd)
Singapore General Hospital (3, A8; ☎ 6321 4113; Level 2, Block 1, Outram Rd)

DENTAL SERVICES

If you chip a tooth munching on a fish head or require emergency treatment, head for the **National Dental Centre** (3, A8; ☎ 6324 8910; 5 Second Hospital Ave); alternatively, consult the *Yellow Pages*, ask at your hotel, or call one of the hospitals listed above.

PHARMACIES
There are pharmacies in most shopping malls and department stores, usually open from 9am to 9pm. For emergencies contact the hospitals listed opposite.

Holidays
New Year's Day 1 January
Chinese New Year January/February (two days); date varies based on lunar calendar.
Good Friday April
Labour Day 1 May
Vesak Day May
National Day 9 August
Hari Raya Puasa October/November; date varies based on Islamic calendar.
Deepavali October; date varies according to the Indian almanac.
Christmas Day 25 December
Hari Raya Haji December/January; date varies based on Islamic calendar.

Internet
Most Internet cafés in Singapore aren't actually cafés: plenty of computers, but no coffee. Many places are gaming centres, so things can get raucous. Many hotels provide Internet access (either in-room connections or business centres); at Changi Airport it's free!

Major Internet service providers such as CompuServe (www.compuserve.com), AOL (www.aol.com) and AT&T (www.attbusiness.net) have dial-up nodes in Singapore. SingTel (www.singtel.com.sg) and StarHub (www.starhub.com) are the two biggest local providers.

Singapore has a network of more than 500 wireless hotspots. Check www.wi-fi hotspotsdirectory.com for details.

INTERNET CAFÉS
Access rates are around $4 per hour.
Chills Cafe (3, D5; ☎ 6883 1016; 01-07 Stamford House, 39 Stamford Rd; ✆ 9.30am-midnight)
Eminent (4, B2; ☎ 6732 0508; 02-21 Far East Shopping Centre, 545 Orchard Rd; ✆ 9am-10pm)

i-surf (4, C1; ☎ 6734 3225; 02-14 Far East Plaza, 14 Scotts Rd; ✆ 11am-11pm)

USEFUL WEBSITES
The Lonely Planet website (www.lonelyplanet.com) offers a speedy link to many of Singapore's websites. Others to try:
Changi International Airport (www.changi.airport.com.sg)
Singapore Government (www.gov.sg)
Singapore Tourism Board (www.visitsingapore.com)
Straits Times (www.straitstimes.asia1.com.sg)
Uberture E-Mag (www.uberture.com) Nightlife, entertainment, shopping, society.

Lost Property
Contact the following:
Changi Airport (☎ Terminal 1 6541 2107, Terminal 2 6541 2222)
MRT train (☎ 1800 336 8900)
SBS Transit bus (☎ 6383 7211)
Tanglin Police Station (☎ 6391 0000)

Metric System
Singapore weighs and measures with the metric system. Clothing-store assistants usually understand both European and US sizes.

TEMPERATURE
$°C = (°F - 32) ÷ 1.8$
$°F = (°C × 1.8) + 32$

DISTANCE
1in = 2.54cm
1cm = 0.39in
1m = 3.3ft = 1.1yd
1ft = 0.3m
1km = 0.62 miles
1 mile = 1.6km

WEIGHT
1kg = 2.2lb
1lb = 0.45kg
1g = 0.04oz
1oz = 28g

VOLUME
1L = 0.26 US gallons
1 US gallon = 3.8L
1L = 0.22 imperial gallons
1 imperial gallon = 4.55L

Money

For tipping and bargaining information see opposite.

CURRENCY

The unit of currency is the Singapore dollar (comprising 100¢). There are 5¢, 10¢, 20¢, 50¢ and $1 coins, while notes come in $2, $5, $10, $50, $100, $500 and $1000 denominations. There's also a $10,000 note (not that we've ever seen one).

TRAVELLERS CHEQUES

Travellers cheques are a good backup when all else fails. You can buy them at Singapore post offices, and sometimes use them instead of cash in shops and restaurants.

CREDIT CARDS

All major credit cards are widely accepted. The tourism authorities suggest that if shops insist on adding a credit-card surcharge (which they shouldn't do), contact the relevant credit company in Singapore. Most hotels and car-hire companies will insist on a credit card and will probably demand full payment upfront if you can't produce one. For 24-hour card cancellations or assistance:

American Express (☎ 6538 4833)
Diners Club (☎ 6294 4222)
MasterCard (☎ 6533 2888)
Visa (☎ 6437 5800)

ATMs

Most ATMs accept MasterCard, Visa and cards with Plus or Cirrus. ATMs are everywhere, including shopping centres and MRT stations.

CHANGING MONEY

You can change money at banks and moneychangers. The major banks (mostly open 9.30am to 3pm Monday to Friday, 9.30am to noon Saturday) line their coffers in the CBD and on Orchard Rd, charging a $2 to $3 service fee. Moneychangers offer better rates, don't charge fees and are located in almost every shopping centre in Singapore; use a licensed operator.

Larger department stores accept foreign cash and travellers cheques at lower rates than you'll get from moneychangers.

Newspapers & Magazines

The press in Singapore is (theoretically) free to assert its opinions, but government crackdowns happen and self-censorship is the norm. International English-language publications such as *Time* and *Newsweek* are readily available. For local news see the *Straits Times* broadsheet or the tabloids *New Paper* and *Today*. For entertainment see *8 Days*, *I-S* and *Juice* magazines. Lifestyle magazines include *Her World* and the stylish *Men's Folio*. *Ex-pat* is suited to long-term visitors. Gourmands should check out Tatler's *Singapore's Best Restaurants*, *Wine & Dine*, or have a look at *Makansutra* for hawker stalls.

Opening Hours

Singapore gets off to a snoozy start, most shops and eateries opening their doors around 10 or 11am. Restaurants often close for the afternoon from 2pm to 6pm. Shops stay open late (10 or 11pm), and night time is the right time for eating – hawker centres keep cooking 'til the early hours. Many small shops, except those in Little India, are closed on Sunday. For post office hours see below, and for banks see left.

Photography & Video

You'll find photo-processing outlets in most shopping malls. For professional services refer to the *Yellow Pages* for locations. Singapore uses the PAL video format, also used in Australia and most of Europe.

Post

Singapore's postal system is predictably efficient, plentiful outlets also provide public phones, packaging materials and financial services. Call ☎ 1605 for the closest branch or try www.signpost.com.sg. Generally post office hours are 8.30am to 5pm Monday to Friday and 8.30am to 1pm Saturday.

Handy outlets include the following:

Changi Airport (2, J3; ☎ public 6542 7899, transit 6543 0048; ☻ 24hr)

Killiney Rd (4, F2; ☎ 6734 7899; 1 Killiney Rd; ☻ 8.30am-9pm Mon-Fri, 8.30am-4pm Sat, 10am-4pm Sun)

Takashimaya (4, D2; ☎ 6738 6899; 04-15 Ngee Ann City, 391 Orchard Rd; ☻ 9.30am-6.30pm Mon-Fri, 9.30am-3pm Sat)

POSTAL RATES

Airmail postcards to anywhere in the world cost $1; letters cost from $1.50 to $2.50.

Radio

English-language radio stations include the BBC World Service (88.9FM), Gold (90.5FM), Symphony (92.4FM), NewsRadio (93.8FM), Class (95FM) and Perfect 10 (98.7FM). Passion (99.5FM) features arts and world music; Power (98FM) aims pop at 18- to 35-year-olds.

Most radio stations have web streaming if you want to get a taste before you come. For iPod owners, www.podcast.net lists dozens of private broadcasters.

Telephone

The country code for Singapore is ☎ 65. You can make local and international calls from public phones – most take phone cards, some take credit cards, while old-school coin booths are rare. For inquiries and information see www.singtel.com.sg. Local phone cards are widely available and offer the cheapest rates.

MOBILE PHONES

Singapore mobile phone numbers start with the digit 9. If you have 'global roaming' facilities with your home provider, your GSM digital phone will automatically tune into one of Singapore's two digital networks (MI-GSM or ST-GSM). There's complete island coverage, and phones also work underground on the MRT.

USEFUL PHONE NUMBERS

International directory inquiries (☎ 104)

International operator (☎ 1635)

Local directory inquiries (☎ 100)

Weather (☎ 6542 7788)

Television

Singapore has five free-to-air channels: Channel 5 (English); Channel 8 (Mandarin); Suria (Malay); Central (English arts, children's programmes and Indian); and Channel News Asia, a news and information channel.

Time

Singapore is eight hours ahead of GMT/UTC, two hours behind Australian Eastern Standard Time (Sydney and Melbourne), 13 hours ahead of American Eastern Standard Time (New York) and 16 hours ahead of American Pacific Standard Time (San Francisco and Los Angeles). At noon in Singapore, the following times apply in these countries: 11pm in New York (the previous day), 8pm in Los Angeles (the previous day), 4am in London, 6am in Johannesburg, 5pm in Auckland and 2pm in Sydney.

Tipping & Bargaining

Tipping is prohibited in the airport and discouraged in major hotels and restaurants, where a 10% service charge is included in the bill. Elsewhere a thank-you tip for good service is discretionary.

Most shops and department stores have fixed prices. Expect to haggle at markets, antique stores and electronics shops where prices aren't displayed.

Tourist Information

Singapore Tourism Board (STB; ☎ 1800 736 2000; www.visitsingapore.com) provides the widest range of services, including tour bookings and event ticketing. There are visitors centres at the following locations (Suntec City is an unmanned info desk):

Changi Airport (2, J3; Terminals 1 & 2; ☻ 6am-2am)

HarbourFront (1, B1; 01-31D
HarbourFront Centre; ⏰ 10am-6pm)
Liang Court (3, C5; L1, Liang Court
Shopping Centre, 177 River Valley Rd;
⏰ 10.30am-9.30pm)
Orchard Rd (4, E2; cnr of Cairnhill &
Orchard Rds; ⏰ 9.30am-10.30pm)
Suntec City (3, E5; L1, Suntec City, 3
Temasek Blvd; ⏰ 10am-6pm)

Women Travellers

Singaporean women enjoy a high degree
of autonomy and respect. Singapore is one
of the safest destinations in Southeast Asia
and sexual harassment is less common than
it probably is in your home country. Women
may find the sheer number of men in Little
India, especially on Sunday night, a little
overwhelming, but again there's really very

little risk. Tampons and contraceptive pills
are readily available.

LANGUAGE

Singapore's official languages are Malay,
Mandarin, Tamil and English; many Singaporeans drift between several of these with
dazzling ease. Most people speak excellent
English, although the elderly and poorly
educated may not. Communication diffi-
culties can arise due to the mutual incom-
prehensibility of each other's accents. To
overcome this, speak slower (not louder),
smile and stay cool – getting excited will
exacerbate the problem. Locals also speak
the colloquial Singlish – a slang mix of
English, Malay and Hokkien. Lonely Planet's *Mandarin Phrasebook* is a useful little
tome.

Index

SIGHTS

SLEEPING

FEATURES

- Kinara — *Eating*
- Shaw Complex — *Entertainment*
- Blue Note — *Drinking*
- Asian Civilisations Museum — *Highlights*
- Raffles City — *Shopping*
- Substation Gallery — *Sights/Activities*
- Sleepy Sam's — *Sleeping*
- Sisters' Islands — *Trips & Tours*

AREAS

- Beach, Desert
- Building
- Land
- Mall
- Other Area
- Park/Cemetery
- Sports
- Urban

HYDROGRAPHY

- River, Creek
- Intermittent River
- Canal
- Swamp
- Water

BOUNDARIES

- State, Provincial
- International
- Disputed

ROUTES

- Tollway
- Freeway
- Primary Road
- Secondary Road
- Tertiary Road
- Lane
- Under Construction
- One-Way Street
- Unsealed Road
- Mall/Steps
- Tunnel
- Walking Path
- Walking Trail/Track
- Pedestrian Overpass
- Walking Tour

TRANSPORT

- Airport, Airfield
- Bus Route
- Cycling, Bicycle Path
- Ferry
- Metro
- Monorail
- Rail
- Cable-Car, Funicular
- Tram
- MRT Station

SYMBOLS

- Bank, ATM
- Beach
- Buddhist Temple
- Castle, Fortress
- Christian
- Embassy, Consulate
- Hindu Temple
- Hospital, Clinic
- Information
- Internet Access
- Mosque
- Lighthouse
- Lookout
- Monument
- Mountain, Volcano
- National Park
- Parking Area
- Petrol Station
- Picnic Area
- Point of Interest
- Police Station
- Post Office
- Swimming Pool
- Telephone
- Toilets
- Waterfall
- Zoo, Bird Sanctuary

24/7 travel advice
www.lonelyplanet.com